Kerry Tucker

After spending four-and-a-half years as an inmate of a maximum-security prison, Kerry Tucker was released with a Master of Arts. She went on to get a doctorate and to become a lecturer at Swinburne University. She currently works for an educational institution in Melbourne and is a passionate advocate for educating women in prison.

Craig Henderson

Craig Henderson has worked as a writer and editor at Australian newspapers, magazines and on-line since 1987. Today the father of three lives on the New South Wales South Coast with his wife, Lizzie.

THE PRISONER

KERRY TUCKER
WITH CRAIG HENDERSON

WILLIAM HEINEMANN: AUSTRALIA

Pseudonyms have been used in this book and other details altered where necessary to protect the identity and privacy of people mentioned.

A William Heinemann book
Published by Penguin Random House Australia Pty Ltd
Level 3, 100 Pacific Highway, North Sydney NSW 2060
penguin.com.au

Penguin
Random House
Australia

First published by William Heinemann in 2018

Addresses for the Penguin Random House group of companies can be found at global.penguinrandomhouse.com/offices.

A catalogue record for this
book is available from the
National Library of Australia

NATIONAL
LIBRARY
OF AUSTRALIA

ISBN 978 0 14379 397 7

Cover background photograph by Bojan Markovic, courtesy of Getty Images
Cover image of prisoner by phoelixDE, courtesy of Shutterstock
Cover design by Louisa Maggio © Penguin Random House Australia Pty Ltd
Internal design by Midland Typesetters, Australia
Typeset in 12/17.5 pt Sabon LT by Midland Typesetters, Australia
Printed in Australia by Griffin Press, an accredited ISO AS/NZS 14001:2004
Environmental Management System printer

Penguin Random House Australia uses papers that are natural, renewable and recyclable products and made from wood grown in sustainable forests. The logging and manufacturing processes are expected to conform to the environmental regulations of the country of origin.

To Shannyn and Sarah.
Without you both, tomorrow wouldn't be
worth the wait and yesterday wouldn't
be worth remembering.

CONTENTS

PROLOGUE

There's a secret nether world under the skyscrapers in the heart of Melbourne. I know because I've been down there. Every day ordinary people walk on top of it as they pass by the marble-panelled Magistrates' Court, the architectural drama of the County Court of Victoria, the imposing sandstone grandeur of the Supreme Court of Victoria and countless buildings in the judicial precinct brimming with law firms and street-level cafes. But few pedestrians know about the labyrinth that exists just a metre or so beneath their feet; nor could they imagine the tide of human wreckage that flows through its hidden passageways day in, day out. I'm damned sure none of them could have known I was entombed under the footpath, how I ended up there or what was to become of me. I was a prisoner. I didn't exist.

During the eighteen months I was remanded in prison while awaiting sentencing for a crime I'll come to a little later, I came to feel oddly comfortable in this strange, subterranean city. Whenever I was brought into the central business district to face court I'd plunge underground into a vast garage, usually with a clutch of other prisoners, in a fortified steel wagon dubbed 'the Brawler'. Once herded out by Corrections Officers, I hardly caught a glimpse of natural light for the rest of the day. If you're an inmate, the beacon of justice flickers out of fluorescent tubes.

The sunken caverns are linked by a network of hall-ways that burrow beneath the busy streets and tramlines, connecting the various court houses and ancillary services to one another. Corridors snake off to conference rooms, administration centres, a fully staffed medical facility and, of course, cells. Here men and women of varying degrees of culpability and criminal pedigree languish until summoned to the wooden docks of the courtrooms in the real world upstairs.

After one short appearance in 2003 I was escorted from the Magistrates' Court back underground and locked in a cell to wait for the Brawler to cart me back to the maximum-security prison on the outskirts of Melbourne that had become my home. Glancing up, I noticed a steel grate through which a ray of sunlight trickled into the cell. Then I saw shapes moving outside; legs and feet flashing by. When I craned my neck I could clearly see the footpath of William Street and the world I'd been removed from more than a year earlier.

'What would they think if they knew there was someone locked in a cage down here looking up at them?' I wondered. 'Would they get down on their hands and knees and try to talk to me? Would they care? What would they say to me? How would I introduce myself? Would I tell them I had once been just like them?'

As I watched Melbournians hurry past my bunker I became transfixed by a pretty woman whose heel had become stuck in one of the footpath's steel grates. Time slowed down and as she bent down to free her trapped shoe my mind took a perfectly sharp, detailed photograph of the moment. I can still see the stitching on her shiny black stiletto heels and the fabric of her tan-coloured skirt. I liked the way it flared, as if she'd just stepped out of the 1950s. Boy, I *really* loved that skirt.

A second later she was free again; heels clicking purposefully as she strutted down William Street. 'Where's she going?' I wondered. 'Is she heading home? Is she married? What's her husband like? Does she have children? Maybe she has little girls like I do? Will she walk through her front door tonight, grab them, smooch them and bundle them into a bathtub full of fragrant bubbles?' Oh, how I missed my own darling cherubs, Shannyn and Sarah.

The smell of their skin and hair, the softness of their little paws in mine. Their smiles. Their tears. Their voices. Their bath time. Their need for Mummy. Their very souls.

I had to be careful – reminiscing was a dangerous indulgence. If I allowed myself to touch my purest emotions about my children – the anguish, longing, guilt, pain and regret – I risked being totally overwhelmed and losing the mental strength to make it through the years of prison that stretched ahead of me. I'd already come too close for comfort a couple of times.

The familiar metallic clank of a key in the oversized lock brought me back to reality. 'OK, time to go,' the Corrections Officer announced flatly as the cell door was opened. The Brawler was fuelled up and about to depart the underworld to take me back to purgatory on the loneliest fringe of the city. There would be no husband and kids waiting when I got there, no welcome-home glass of vino. Instead I'd be eating sandwiches behind razor wire with a woman who'd stabbed her husband to death and another who'd suffocated her children with a pillow.

As I lay awake on my prison mattress that night I silently reaffirmed the vow I'd made to my girls – and to myself – over and over in the depth of my heart. 'I will make you proud of me again. One day I will leave this place and you will be proud that I am your mummy. I promise.'

It would prove easier said than done.

1

RISE AND FALL

'Forgive me, Father, for I have sinned.'

And then – silence.

As a little girl I'd murmur those mildewed words into my lap once a week, hunched over in the stuffy confessional booth at St Joseph's Catholic Church. Nine times out of ten I'd leave it at that, unable to go on.

'Y-*e-e-e-s-s-s*?' the priest would eventually prompt me in the hope of unleashing a torrent of heinous admissions from the perplexed and frightened ten-year-old on the other side of the screen.

'Well, Father, the thing is I can't actually think of anything that I've done wrong,' I'd explain, nervously. 'Unless you count how I just told you now to "forgive me for I have sinned" because that was pretty much a lie so maybe that's the sin you can forgive me for?'

I was at once bemused and entranced by the Catholic Church and its odd customs and totems, its crusty old men and the torturous, endless boredom of Mass. To me the idea of pretending to drink someone's blood and chew on his skin of a Sunday was downright freaky. So was having to confess to 'sins' all the time when I knew perfectly well I'd lived my first decade within the confines of the Ten Commandments – at least the ones I understood. I hadn't killed anyone, I hadn't committed adultery (whatever that was), I hadn't coveted thy neighbours' goods (whatever that meant) and I hadn't stolen, although I did know what stealing was.

I don't think I ever believed in a god, Jesus, a holy ghost or any kind of saint, but for some reason I still took comfort in the processes of the church. I was a Catholic because my mum and dad were Catholics – big time Catholics. My Dad, Jim Larkin, was an Irishman by descent and particularly committed to the church. Our home in Leeton – a pastured expanse in the lush food-growing region of south-western New South Wales – was where local priests came to get drunk. On Friday nights our laundry was virtually a clergy clubhouse. Kegs of beer would be tapped as old men in holy garb hunkered down around our wash tub and baskets of clothes. Drinking with Mum and Dad to all hours was apparently part of their job. And they wanted *me* to ask for forgiveness?

I think Dad was wedded to his faith as much by his strong Irish roots as he was by the church's love of a booze-up. After moving from Rosebery in Tasmania, he took up a position as an accountant and manager at the Leeton Cannery. Dad was one of those guys other men respected; people looked up to him and it was clear, even as a layman, that he held sway among the priests. Although he made his children front up to church every week, he was by no means pious. There was no particular morality pushed on us at home; nor were there any lofty or unreasonable rules enforced. Dad was pretty cool.

He did, however, make us all go to confession. St Joseph's Church in Leeton wasn't the biggest building in Australia, but to a little girl like me it was as cavernous and imposing as St Paul's Cathedral. I felt as if I was going to be fed to the lions whenever I was ushered towards that confessional booth. 'Forgive me, Father, for I have sinned – but not really! I haven't done anything wrong! Honestly.' It truly used to annoy those arbiters of good and evil. Sometimes, to grease the tracks of righteousness, the priests were backgrounded with pre-fabricated 'sins' prepared earlier by my mother, Colleen. '*Nothing* to confess, child? Didn't you steal your sister's basketball shorts?' the Father would venture.

'Oh yeah, that,' I'd splutter, wondering how he even knew, and thinking he'd definitely stretched the definition of 'stealing' near to breaking point. 'Forgive me, Father, for I borrowed my sister's basketball shorts without asking.' By my early teens I'd taken to conjuring fake sins from thin air just so we could all get on with it. 'Forgive me, Father, for I stole some feather dusters from school.' No matter what crime I had committed against God, I was always sentenced to 100 Hail Marys. I had to sit in the pews and recite them, and I never cheated or skimped at fifty, partly because, well, that was the punishment, and partly because I thought the priests might be watching. Maybe they were.

By the time I was in high school we'd moved more than 350 kilometres away to Robinvale and onto a whole new clique of drunken holy men. Decades later I'd hear the names of some of the priests who used to frequent our home mentioned in news reports about the Royal Commission into Institutional Responses to Child Sexual Abuse. Confession indeed.

Robinvale is an unremarkable fruit-growing region on the banks of the Murray River in far north-west Victoria. Dad had taken a job managing the finances of farmers through the local growers Co-Op, and he made a big footprint in a little town. Mum was a homemaker, though for some reason she never had the time – or the desire – to make me feel at home. She once told me, without a hint of regret, that when I was born she couldn't be bothered thinking of a name for me. She overheard somebody call out for a Kerry in the hospital ward and thought, 'That'll do.' I might as well have been named after Kerry Packer.

I never knew my maternal grandparents but I'll never forget my dad's mother, mainly because she hated my guts. I hated hers right back to make things nice and square. I thought she was a witch; she had a wart on her chin with hairs growing out of it and everything. We six kids (two boys and four girls) would visit her in Geelong, where she and her second husband raised greyhounds at an old house that had a toilet way down deep in the backyard. Despite being the second youngest, if I needed to pee in the middle of the night Grandma would force me to go out there alone, scared witless, while the others kids were all allowed to use a bucket inside. She consistently singled me out. 'You're just like your father,' the old crone would hiss. It was obviously meant as an insult, which I could never understand because everybody knew Dad was a wonderful man.

I was fifteen when he died in 1979. I came home one afternoon to see paramedics loading Dad into the back of an ambulance in our driveway. Later that night he was airlifted by helicopter to a bigger hospital in Melbourne. They said he'd had a cerebral haemorrhage. At 2am the phone rang and when I heard Mum scream I knew he was gone.

After Dad died, everything started to fall apart. My four older siblings had married and left home by then so only my younger brother and I remained in the care of our clearly malfunctioning mother. In the immediate aftermath of our devastating loss, one thing overshadowed all else. His name was Uncle Johnny. He was Dad's older brother, though he looked identical. They appeared the same in every way except that Johnny was an evil sexual deviant who preyed on his own daughter – my lovely cousin Cathy. Johnny came to Dad's funeral and then saw fit to park himself in our house where he proceeded to get extremely gropey with me. My big brother and brothers-in-law told him to back off or they were going to sort him out. Thankfully he's dead now.

Poor cousin Cathy, however, had no brotherly protectors. She was a stunningly beautiful girl who was stabbed to death in a beachside car park near Wollongong, New South Wales, by a guy called Jeffrey Upfold in an apparent argument over drugs. She was just twenty-two. Cathy had become a heroin addict and no one need guess why, after being raped by her monster of a father for years. Still, the last time I saw Cathy I was shocked to see what had happened to her. She had gone from being a strong, black-haired beauty to a white, scabbed-over stick insect with her hair in rats tails. Someone had to say to me, 'This is your cousin, Cathy! Remember?' Her devolution from gorgeous to ghostly had a profound and instructive impact on me: it put me off taking drugs of any kind for life.

Substance abuse in our little universe revolved around Mum and the demon drink. Mum was an alcoholic and she only grew worse after Dad died. She'd start in the morning and sip away all day until she was a complete mess. We'd find empty cans everywhere; behind the couch, under tables – even under her bed.

I'm sure Mum used alcohol as an emotional crutch. She had relied on Dad for everything. We all did. Before he died I always thought we were well off. We lived in a nice house in a nice street and Dad was the consummate professional man. As kids we never wanted for much, but the hard truth – revealed like a twist in the plot when he died – was that Dad was just about bankrupt. As well as an accountant, he also happened to be an SP bookmaker and had amassed enough gambling debt to sink a battleship. He had no savings, no investments, no life insurance: nothing. He left Mum high and dry.

People from the Co-Op soon turned up at our house and took back the car. They went through my parents' bedroom, gawking at files and taking papers away. All of a sudden people who only a week earlier had been warm and respectful, were hostile. The upshot was that Mum had to go out and work. She managed to stay sober long enough to hold down a job managing the front office at the local supermarket, but a year or so later she quit and crawled back inside the bottle. I had no such place to hide.

2

THE WONDER YEARS

Being an 'intelligent' kid can have its ups and downs. In my case, it saw me elevated by two full academic years – from year nine to year eleven – in one year. For some reason, schoolwork, exams and problem-solving came easily to me. On the downside, being brainy left me somewhat isolated. Suddenly, I was in a strange teenage no-man's-land, removed from my peers and with hormonal chaos in full swing. I'm pretty sure people considered me a smarty pants, too. I guess it would have been hard not to.

The resulting disconnection made it harder for me to bind with a group, or even individuals, but to be honest I had always struggled to belong and in some ways I was used to being alone. From a young age I had wandered through life sort of bumping off things; I never connected and instead nudged into people only to be deflected onto another trajectory. It's not as though I sat at home alone – I *did* have a social life of sorts. Robinvale was a strong sporting town and I was right into basketball, but I moved through myriad groups and never stuck to anyone in particular, and no one stuck to me. I never had that slam-dunk best friend.

There was one way, though, that I was a bit of a hit: with the boys. All the Larkin girls had been. But even then it seemed as though I had some sort of Teflon coating. While teenagers in our town would pair up and become an item, have a little relationship, hold hands, be together, whatever – that never happened with me. Not for a long time. Boys were interested in me, for sure, but it was clear they just wanted to have a sexual experience and nothing else. No romance, no relationship, no holding hands, no chit-chat. What made it all the more confounding was that I wouldn't let them use me like that: I didn't sleep around. I just couldn't understand why, then, they seemed to think of me as little more than boobs, a bum and a pretty face.

A few years later this type of treatment escalated. 'He's out there again,' I'd yell out to Mum when the fat, ugly fifty-something-year-old man was standing outside my bedroom window at night, leering through the curtains. The creep would also come in to the local refrigeration company where I had a receptionist's job, and bring little presents or stand at the door and ogle me. Once he even said, 'I liked what you were wearing to bed last night.' It didn't take long for word to get around and he was barred from the premises. The refrigeration mechanics promised they'd always protect me and break his head if necessary. But after dark he would sneak around as he pleased and so in the end I spoke privately to some policemen I knew. They didn't muck around; they bashed him with a phone book and I never saw him again.

Almost as upsetting as being the target of a stalker was Mum's reaction. To her, the whole thing had been a giant hassle. It annoyed her. *I* annoyed her. 'Oh, for God's sake, you bring these things on yourself, Kerry! Get over it,' she'd moan. The insinuation was that if it wasn't for the fact that I existed, the man wouldn't have to perv on me. I came to thoroughly resent my mother, and her indifference to my being stalked was just one of many reasons why.

Losing my virginity, in one sense, was as earth-shattering as losing a set of keys. To me, crossing the great sexual boundary was as routine as being selected for the under 15s basketball team or passing a school maths test.

In Robinvale, one's first sexual encounter was more a rite of passage than a sacred or special occasion. But, as far as blokes go, Terry wasn't a bad choice for my first time. It's not as though he wooed me with a candle-lit dinner or swept me off my feet to a bed strewn with rose petals. No, like a lot of clueless Aussie girls of that era, my virginity went missing somewhere in the back of a Holden panel van.

I was fourteen when Terry and I became an item. I'd met him after a mutual friend suggested we'd be a good fit. It turned out we were. Sort of. He was a happy-go-lucky eighteen-year-old who came across as a surfy dude in spite of Robinvale being 497 kilometres from the nearest beach. Somehow Terry pulled it off. As a bonus to his relative good looks, he also treated me well and wanted to spend time with me outside of all the pashing and fondling.

For a year or so I'd been half-pretending that I'd already had sex, believing this brought me social standing and validated me as a 'woman of the world'. Whenever girls tittered about high adventures in the bedroom or EH Holden station wagon, I'd snigger, nod and laugh as if to say, 'Oh my *God*! I know what you mean!' Of course, I had virtually no clue about sex. I was a naive kid and as far as I was concerned the birds were magpies and the bees were dodgy stinging insects. But I'd listen to tales – not knowing whether they were true or not – of how girls my age had lost their virginity, and I thought it was high time I joined the club. I desperately wanted to fit in. Once Terry was on the scene, it was just a matter of time.

Because it was quasi-procedural in country towns like ours, having sex for the first time was anything but intimate. In fact, it was a full-on community event. You could have sold tickets or set up a sausage sizzle alongside and made a killing. The location was usually the same – the Robinvale Drive-in. It was all pre-arranged and everyone knew what was going to happen. I'm surprised there wasn't an ad in the local paper.

When the fateful Friday night rolled around, Terry didn't have his own car so a kindly young gent by the name of Spider loaned us his panel van, which was parked in a suitably dim corner of the drive-in. The whole thing was such a contrivance that I felt like Sandy in a scene from *Grease!* All the boys mooched on one side and the girls clucked and giggled on the other, and when Terry and I climbed into the panel van – replete with a rather mangy mattress – the fellas went one way and the dames walked off in the other direction.

I guess the Holden jiggled about on its springs for a while but the earth definitely did *not* move for me. When it was all over – pretty quickly, I might add – I couldn't understand what all the fuss and hype had been about. I thought sexual intercourse was a complete non-event. But at least I'd ticked the box and was no longer a lowly virgin. The only problem was that, suddenly, Terry wanted nothing to do with me. You'd think he'd be chuffed but the very next day he was in a mighty huff. I had absolutely no idea what I'd done to deserve it, especially since he'd shown me such a good time in Spider's five-star rusty Holden. I wasn't too pleased about being cast aside like one of my mum's empty beer cans. I was a pretty fiery, headstrong little thing and I demanded his respect.

Finally, I tracked Terry down late in the afternoon at someone's house where he was hanging out with his brother and a few mates. 'What's the matter with you?' I demanded. 'Why are you avoiding me? Why won't you speak to me? I thought we were together!'

After a long pause, Terry worked up the nerve to explain. It turned out he felt betrayed. Wounded in fact. *Deceived.* 'Because you're not really a virgin!' he spat. '*That's* why!'

I knew perfectly well that until about 9pm the previous night I had most definitely been a virgin. I might as well have been named Mary and arrived at the drive-in on a mule. 'Yes I am . . . or I *was* until you showed up!' I exploded in disbelief. 'What in the fuck are you talking about? I mean, how would you even know that?'

'Because you didn't bleed,' Terry sneered accusingly.

'What? I didn't know I was supposed to.'

'If you're a virgin, you bleed,' Prince Charming insisted.

'Well, maybe your dick wasn't big enough,' I suggested helpfully.

The remark cut deep and Terry's brother shot me an admiring look that said, 'Oh, you're *quick*!' If Terry was wounded by my lack of virgin blood, he was crushed by my jibe about his manhood – particularly in front of his brother and their giggling mates. But I wouldn't have had to resort to belittling him like that had he not first embarrassed me with his public dissection of the virtues of my vaginal discharge. I'd been humiliated and my only recourse was to destroy him emotionally. So I did. It was a technique that would later come in handy when I was in maximum security.

Within about a month Terry and I were back on talking terms – and more. Nowadays I shudder at the memory, but I would go to his place almost every lunchtime in my school uniform and have sex in the shed. It was a horrible shed, too – even worse than Spider's car. At sixteen I fell pregnant. I knew something wasn't right, so one day I paid a visit to a doctor who also happened to be a very dear friend of my late father's. After a quick test and examination he sat me down and looked at me with an expression that was a sour cocktail of disappointment, pity and contempt.

'Well, you *are* pregnant,' he said with a shake of his head. 'I hope you're proud of yourself.' It was as if I was a dog that had just soiled itself on the carpet. But Dr Denigration was only getting started. 'I just thank God your father isn't around to see this. Oh, and look at what you've done to your mother! This is the last thing she needs.'

In less than a minute I had shrunk from being Terry's girl back into being Daddy's little girl – the one who was being told I had just disrespected the very memory of him. For the first time I could remember I had a distinct feeling I was in way over my head. 'Wait here,' the doctor instructed before stepping into another office to phone Mum. After a muffled conversation he came back into the surgery. 'Your mother is aggrieved and you are making her life harder,' he curtly informed me before launching into a protracted rant about what a selfish, stupid and 'loose' little girl I was. Who was I to argue with a grown-up – and one of Dad's best mates, no less?

'Here's what happens if you're pregnant when you're as young as you are,' he continued. 'We do a procedure to make sure everything is OK – to ensure that your body is working properly. Your mother and I have agreed that I'll be able to do that tonight.'

A few hours later I was wearing a surgical gown at a hospital while the doctor and an anaesthetist conferred without addressing me once. When I woke up a little while later, I was informed that I was no longer pregnant. They had 'fixed' it. I was mortified. I'd had no idea about their secret plot to abort the baby growing inside me; I was told it was a routine 'check-up'. I boiled with resentment towards my mother and the medicos. I felt violated, betrayed and invaded. They had conspired to drug me, shove steel instruments inside me and suck pieces out. Pieces of another person without so much as a by-your-leave.

Looking back, there hadn't been time for me to think, 'Do I want this baby?' I hadn't even had the chance to discuss it with Terry! It was all done and dusted before I could catch a breath. The emotional odyssey from 'I think I might be pregnant' to 'Yes, you are. You're an idiot, but don't worry because we've killed it' was about six hours.

By this time, Terry and I had been together a couple of years and if I'd had the chance to talk it over with him properly I'm pretty sure he would have wanted to have the baby. He was that kind of guy. Maybe I would have been swayed. It remains a great big 'What if?' Maybe Terry and I would have settled down. He had a tip-truck business and he was good to me. It might have been great or it might have been a disaster – but that decision was taken out of our hands and I loathed my mother for it.

As for the good doctor? That night in hospital I suffered an almighty haemorrhage. He had royally stuffed up his self-regulated, unilateral, unethical abortion and I was transferred to a larger hospital to stem the flow. I had to undergo a barrage of corrective surgeries to my uterus and womb because he'd botched things so thoroughly that I was told I would never have children. Apparently that was my all my own fault too.

3

MISSING

Terry and I stayed together and one night things got serious pretty quickly. We were at the newly opened Robin-vale Community Arts Centre for the footy end-of-season bash when our best mates Glen and Colleen suddenly took to the stage and grabbed the mic. 'We'd like to formally announce to everyone here tonight that we're engaged to be married!'

Yaaay! Woohoo! Clapping. Wolf whistles and wild, drunken cheering. Once the applause subsided and another wave of beer and champagne had washed through the club, people turned to me and Terry and slurred, 'Youse guys should get engaged, too!'

We looked at each other. 'D'ya think?' I asked Terry.

Terry looked taken aback. 'Dunno, Kerry. D'ya reckon we should?'

'I suppose so,' I replied. 'What do *you* think?'

Terry smiled. 'Oh, yeah, fucken alright! Do you wanna get married?'

'Oh yeah,' I said laughing, 'I guess so!'

So after an hour of umm-ing and ahh-ing we were up onstage, engaged and soaking up the considerably drunker applause, good wishes and cries of 'Terry and Kerry *forev-ahhh*!'

In a small town, news travels like the wind so by 11pm my mother and all my sisters knew about my rapid-fire engagement. 'What are you thinking? You don't decide to get married after five minutes of thought!' they lectured me.

'I didn't,' I shot back. 'I thought about it for an hour!'

I had even taken some quiet time off on my own, while the band was on a break and the best and fairest awards were being announced, to consider the implications of being Terry's wife. I came to the conclusion I could make a go of it. Six months later – before we'd lifted a finger to plan our wedding – Terry took off to Darwin for an extended holiday with a couple of mates from Robinvale. When he returned, he brought back with him the most adorable souvenir – a new fiancee by the name of Simone.

'Obviously it's over between you and me,' he said.

'Oh, do you think?' I replied.

I wasn't at all heartbroken by the turn of events. We were both growing up and apart and our relationship had clearly run its course. I look back at myself at that age and see a kid who felt destined to hook up with the first person who showed long-term interest in her – even though I always tried to project the opposite image. Despite all the things I'd been through, by the time I turned eighteen I was still a naive, vulnerable girl. I had no experience with money, I had no idea of stability or somewhere to call home. The only long-term experience I'd had with men was with Terry and that had been a twisted and tangled journey that really left me none-the-wiser and – apparently – barren.

I'd walk past arcades and milk-bars where kids played pinball machines and think the noisy contraptions were a metaphor for my life. I was the shiny silver ball ricocheting off the bumpers and the harsh realities of life.

In towns like Robinvale being eighteen was like being thirty-five. Back then girls had two choices: you could either marry in the town and settle down to have a family or you could leave and go to Melbourne to become a police officer or a nurse. All of my sisters were married at eighteen and had kids by twenty. As far as I could see they were on a fast track to middle-age – a slightly depressing and horrifying notion. Now that I wasn't getting married to Terry, I was at a loose end, drifting along just waiting for something to happen. I had dropped out of school halfway through year twelve and was working at the refrigeration firm. I was going nowhere fast, or so I thought.

Then I was abducted.

One day Mum organised for me to visit some family friends, Geoff and Judy. They owned a car repair business where I'd done some work, and I'd babysit their kids now and then. On this particular day I was supposed to go to their house after work for dinner. Geoff swung by to pick me up and when I climbed into his car he said we had to collect his young son from football practice. 'Sure, no worries,' I said.

I almost didn't notice as Geoff drove straight past the football fields. He kept driving, and driving. Confused, and increasingly wary, I asked him what was going on and he just said that my mum and the family had organised a little getaway for me and not to worry. I looked around inside the car and noticed a large bag behind Geoff's seat that looked a lot like one of Mum's.

It was well and truly after dark when we pulled up at a road house. There Geoff handed me over to a couple of strangers – two Greek guys. Then he turned around and drove off while the Greek guys put me in their car and headed to a country town a few hundred kilometres away from Robinvale. For the next three months I was virtually held captive by these people – primarily one of them – and forced to live in a house with his wife and two kids and work in his restaurant. When I wasn't waiting on tables I was literally locked in a bedroom. I didn't have a single phone conversation and no one explained why I was there or what it was all about. No one came looking for me. In fact, back in Robinvale, no one really noticed or cared I was missing. Years later my younger brother said he'd always figured I'd 'just run away'.

At night I dressed in a pink uniform, put on pink eye shadow and served customers in the restaurant. The customers would often say how lovely I looked. The place had a large tape deck on the back counter and I would constantly play 'Dancing on the Ceiling' by Lionel Richie loudly. I'd be told to turn it down but the song was an escape for me – I could think of better things when I was listening to it. Nowadays whenever I hear it I get a chill up my spine.

I was in servitude to these random acquaintances of family friends for three months before I thought 'enough is enough' and escaped by climbing out of the bathroom window and boarding a bus to Melbourne. I found out later that I'd been sent away to work in order to 'give Mum a break'. She'd been struggling for years and was trying to look after my younger brother. He'd grown a little rebellious – he was a bit of a drinker and fighter to boot. He'd been prevented from attending Dad's funeral because he'd been deemed too young at the time, and carried a lot of anger back then because he'd been denied the chance to say goodbye.

In Melbourne I linked up with an older girl named Anne – one of the girls in high school who I'd befriended when I moved up a couple of classes. We weren't exactly close but at least I knew her. Anne worked in the city in a shop that sold coats, hats and gloves and she let me stay with her at a little house in Caulfield. After a fairly uneventful three months in the big smoke, I decided to go back 'home'. But in the six months since I climbed into the car to 'go to Geoff and Judy's for dinner', Mum had changed her phone number and moved to a smaller, cheaper house in Mildura ninety kilometres north-west of Robinvale. I shed a tear when I realised she hadn't even bothered to give me her new number.

Robinvale was changing and shutting down. There were better job prospects elsewhere and a few of my older siblings had moved on. So I, too, left behind the town I'd grown up in, played basketball in, got pregnant in, had a forced abortion in, got engaged in, got stalked in and got abducted from, and headed to Mildura – the town I'd get raped in.

4

TEMPEST

I got my own flat in Mildura – the very first place that was all mine. I'd scored an admin job at a local business, but that came to an abrupt end after the owner took me out for a bite to eat at a restaurant nearby. Like the peeping Tom before him, Reg was an unappealing, middle-aged man. They had something else in common, too; both considered me their sexual plaything.

I was oblivious to this when Reg invited me out for lunch on my own one weekday and proceeded to get me blind drunk. Even though I ended up near paralytic from the Bacardi and Cokes he kept plying me with, I'll never forget what happened next. 'I'm feeling sick,' I slurred to Reg, who I had no reason whatsoever to mistrust. When it was obvious I could hardly stand he helped me to my feet, steadied me and walked me out of the restaurant. 'I don't think you should come back to work,' he said. 'Tell me where you live and I'll drive you home, luv.'

Still trusting my new boss – a well-known and respected figure in town – I let him bundle me into his car. 'That'd be great,' I replied boozily. 'I'd love a lift home. Hey, I'm not in trouble for this, am I?' He said no and laughed, maybe because he knew just how much strife I was about to be in. After Reg helped me unlock the door to my unit and closed it behind us, he wasted no time in systematically raping me. He was like a sexual assault machine. I was in a state of total shock – I couldn't believe what was happening to me. I tried to fight him off but my Bacardi-numbed arms and legs were no match for the terrifying strength of a powerfully built man.

The disgusting violation, the crushing fear, the shame and the realisation I was helpless were devastating. The only thing I can smile about today when I think back to Reg is how I threw up all over him mid-assault. I wonder how he explained *that* suspicious stain to his wife. I also pondered whether I was the first victim, the last or just one in a long line of vulnerable young women he attacked – because that animal sure as hell knew what he was doing the day he sank his fangs into me.

A few years later I was living in Melbourne when the police came knocking to ask me about Reg. Other women had come forward and my name had been mentioned as a potential witness. I told the detectives about my traumatic encounter but declined to go on the record in a case against Reg because, while I felt sorry for the other victims, I knew it would be his word against mine and the court process would be humiliating. There was no comfort in knowing I wasn't the only one who was raped. In fact, a few years later I'd come to know just how depressingly common that kind of violation was when I found myself living in a community of women where the rate of rape victims was pretty much 100 per cent.

I've never been too good with dates but I remember the day that the man who would later become my husband convinced me to move to Melbourne and live with him. I know this because as soon as I put the phone down from talking to him I glanced at the TV to see the space shuttle *Challenger* explode in the blue skies off the coast of Florida. They played it over and over again; a speeding fireball, then runaway booster rockets corkscrewing out of control, and then the remains of a spacecraft and seven poor souls raining down onto the hard skin of the Atlantic Ocean as their family members watched in horrified disbelief. It proved to be somewhat emblematic of our relationship.

I'd met him at the Bridge Hotel's nightclub in Mildura during the previous June long weekend. I was out on the town having a couple of drinks with one of my sisters, Lynette. I was still feeling like that bloody pinball, thudding into corners and trapped beneath the glass. I was just waiting for something or someone to happen. My sister and I had gone to an ATM but it was out of money, which put our night at the Bridge in jeopardy. 'Don't worry,'

I told her, 'I'll get someone to buy us drinks.' As soon as we arrived back at the nightclub my future husband was the first person we ran into. He looked like a reasonably pleasant man and said I had a nice arse. I said, 'If that's the case then you can buy me a drink.' He shouted my sister and me a few rounds and we had a decent time. Before we went our separate ways that night I thanked him for the drinks. 'I'm going to be at the Grand Hotel on Sunday having lunch with my sister,' I added. 'If you want me to pay you back, come along.'

He turned up on the Sunday right on the stroke of midday. He was a plumber from Melbourne but from time to time he'd come up north to work in the local wineries. He was a single man, tall, blond, reasonably good looking and a little bit pudgy – the complete opposite of what I'm normally attracted to. But he fussed over me and treated me like I was special. It was winter when we started to become an item during his visits from Melbourne and the range of really nice jumpers he wore made him look safe and normal.

Six months after the *Challenger* blew up I arrived in Melbourne to start my life with him. I had ummed and ahhed about making the move but in the end the clincher came from one of my sisters. 'Don't do it, Kerry,' she warned me. 'I don't like him.'

And that was that – as defiant and strong-willed as ever, I packed up my life and moved to the city to a tiny little flat in Ivanhoe. Just before we left he said he had something to tell me. 'Kerry, I'm actually not single – technically. I'm married and I have two young sons.'

Stunned silence.

'Look, Kerry, I'm not single but I'm *going* to be – soon! We're separated and we're going to get a divorce.'

More silence.

'My boys are with my wife . . . I mean, my ex, at the moment. I just thought I'd better tell you.'

'Oh,' was all I could manage.

It was a mind-blowing revelation. I could almost deal with the soon-to-be ex-wife-situation; at least she was going to be out of his life, according to his account. But the fact he had two little boys was hard to get my head around. I'd had no idea they existed, and the notion of him as a father was alien – an entirely different facet to him that didn't fit in the picture I had of us. *Two little boys?* You've got to be kidding me!

After the shock wore off I mostly felt fearful and vulnerable, but also determined to find a way forward. I'd given up my flat and the job I'd taken working in a motel so the only option was to go back to Mum. I'd rather have stayed in Melbourne and been a step-mother to a dozen random little boys than deal with being her live-in daughter.

I wasn't the only one he deceived. His wife apparently had no idea their marriage was even in trouble. The furore that followed was horrible and I felt trapped and terrified that he would go back to her and leave me stranded in the big, strange city all on my own. He kept flitting between us for about six months before his wife finally kicked him out for good. As ridiculous as it seems now, I got really frightened and clung to the relationship even more and hoped that some calmer water lay ahead. I had rationalised the situation by then and saw it as akin to him splitting up from a girlfriend. I didn't understand the complexity of marriage, divorce and kids. But oh, I would learn all about *that* stuff. Boy, would I learn!

I totally loved Little River Band and when I was browsing a brochure about a P&O cruise to the South Pacific about a year later, the fact they were booked as the ship's entertainment sealed the deal. We weren't yet married but we were keen to try a cruise so we decided to spend up and make the fourteen-day odyssey a romantic 'pre-honeymoon' complete with swaying palm trees, golden sunsets and the languid strum of ukuleles. Those bastards in Little River Band pulled out of the cruise contract after we booked and we got stuck aboard the *Fairstar* with a Country and Western yodeller instead. By the time we docked in Fiji everyone was ready to throw him overboard. But horrible music wasn't the only risk to his safety, or ours: the *Fairstar* had to dodge not one but two tropical cyclones as we lurched around the South Pacific like a drunken lady in heels.

We missed multiple ports due to flooding and instead bobbed on the high seas for days while the storms pounded some poor lost paradise just over the horizon. Everyone was confined indoors because the ship was listing so much in the massive swell that it was too dangerous to go out on deck. After we finally limped into Fiji things went from bad to worse. A military coup was brewing – complete with rebels firing rifles into the air – and a group of us narrowly escaped being robbed in a side alley by locals during the Government-ordered curfew. Then my future husband contracted the crippling diarrhoea that was sweeping through the ship and couldn't leave our cabin.

It didn't stop me; I was still intent on going sightseeing. A group of us disembarked on Dravuni Island, and somehow we ended up getting separated from the ship. It seemed the crew had moved it to the lee side of the island ahead of the impending cyclone. We finally made it back to the *Fairstar* and were ferried out to the ship aboard local pontoon boats that rose and fell on the heaving seas against the *Fairstar*'s massive steel hull. As we pulled alongside, a deckhand had his fingers severed when the shuttle collided with the *Fairstar*. One of the poor man's mangled digits plopped on the deck right at my feet. 'Oh God, that would have hurt!' was all I could say as another local helped me clamber back aboard the cruise liner.

A media scrum was waiting for us when we sailed back into Sydney – such was the news of the ill-fated voyage from hell. We had missed something like eight ports and instead become marooned at sea, where we'd started to run out of food and had long since run out of Coke for my Bacardi. It turned out the guys in Little River Band had made the right call. Good for them. Yet amid all this drama at sea – the sickness and the injuries, the attempted robbery, the gunfire, the flooding and lashing rain, the severing of fingers and the near murder of the world's worst yodeller – these were not the things that my future husband was most annoyed about. No, the thing that really pissed him off was my apparent lack of interest in his sons. 'You know what shits me?' he sulked as we slowly steamed towards the embrace of the Australian coastline. 'You haven't once asked me about the boys this whole trip.'

5

MOTHERHOOD

If I'm honest those boys meant virtually nothing to me back then. It would take time for me to grow close to them and to see them as the wonderful men I care about today. At the time I didn't know who they were, other than the children of the woman their father had secretly cheated on with me.

They were three and five when I moved from Mildura to join their 'single' dad in Melbourne. For some reason he was always at me to kiss them goodnight whenever they stayed over with us, but I thought it weird: kissing strange kids. They weren't part of my life as far as I was concerned – they were just these boys who'd turn up every now and again, and I hated being forced to do things. I had no idea about getting into a relationship with a married man with children, or what the expectations were. I soon learned what his were.

One night quite early in the piece, the boys were staying with us when one of them threw up all over his bed in the spare room. Instinctively I plucked him out of the mess and brought him into our bed. His father was furious. 'If he's thrown up in his own bed, then he'll throw up in *this* bed as well!' he barked.

I raised my voice in return and bit back with a smart-arsed remark. I can't recall exactly what he said but I can still feel his angry reaction like it was yesterday. It left me stunned and my brain struggling to process.

'W-what the fuck was *that*?' I finally stammered.

My crime had been yelling at him in front of his boys. A big no-no apparently. But what followed was an incredible outpouring of love, tenderness and remorse. 'Oh babe, please forgive me,' he cooed, wrapping me in his arms. 'If only you could understand that these are my *sons*. Oh God, I'm so sorry.' I found out later this kind of behaviour was called 'the princess syndrome'. Whatever they labelled it, it certainly worked on me; from the get-go I started thinking any issues with the boys had to be my fault. I wasn't understanding enough. I wasn't being nice enough. I see it differently nowadays, but at the time I was thinking, 'I will be better. I will learn how to look after the kids when they're here. That's what a normal, good person would do.'

Another option, in hindsight, would have been to walk away from the guy, but I went ahead and married him anyway. When things were good between us it could be great, so I concentrated on the good stuff. I could always tell his mood by listening to the sound his feet made when he walked along the concrete, or crunched up the gravel path outside our home and know whether I'd have to walk on eggshells or not. He had his happy feet on the day he proposed to me – the very same day his divorce came through from his first wife. He presented me with a ring and said, 'Will you marry me?'

'Of course,' I said. 'No problem.'

Given the harbingers of our relationship to that point it's needless to say the wedding was a complete disaster – mostly thanks to me. From the outset I was fixated on outdoing his ex-wife. If she'd had a fleet of white Ford Fairlanes, I had to have gleaming white Jaguars. He once remarked that her wedding dress had cost $800 so I made sure mine cost $1200. She'd had one bridesmaid so I had two. She had a flower girl so I had a flower girl *and* a ring-bearer. I was the Bridezilla of all Bridezillas.

I took control of everything: I booked the venue, an exclusive little German-themed place in Lilydale that had a chapel and glockenspiel bells. I chose the date, the Friday of the Australia Day long weekend in 1990 – not realising I had messed up the dates so we were in fact getting married *on* Australia Day. Oh yeah, and it was 43 degrees in the shade. My $1200 dress weighed twenty kilos, the beer was hot, and Mum was pissed and staggering all over the place as we were about to go down the aisle. At the last minute I asked my older brother to please walk me down the aisle instead of Mum.

'What are you asking me for?' he responded.

'Because Mum's pissed and she can't do it!' I hissed as the embarrassed guests waited politely in the pews while we discussed it at the chapel door. It was just chaos. Somehow we managed to exchange vows, but as the boiling beer and warm wine flowed into the evening, the family arguments escalated. I was actually glad to be called Tucker and not Larkin anymore. As far as weddings go, mine was the absolute worst I have ever been to. If I'd booked Little River Band they would have cancelled on me to play onboard some P&O cruise instead.

Not content with just an ill-suited marriage, after the wedding my husband and I decided to work together. We ran a number of hotels and ended up managing the Lake Hume Resort in Albury–Wodonga near the NSW–Victoria border.

Over the years I had forged a decent career out of working in and co-managing hotels, motels and little resorts along the highways and byways of rural New South Wales and Victoria. It wasn't what I had planned on. As a little girl I'd always wanted to be a vet. When I realised I didn't really like animals all that much I thought I could be a police officer instead. I even travelled down to Melbourne after I'd quit school and met with the police recruiters, but I was either two inches too short or five kilos too heavy to qualify for whatever the minimum physical standard was back in the day. Their loss.

So, after a series of small jobs and false starts, I found myself settling into the travel accommodation industry. Over several years I helped run businesses in Mildura, Healesville, Yarrawonga, Wagga Wagga and Albury–Wodonga. I liked the work – it was busy, consistent, stable – and I had racked up some funny stories along the way, like when I was quite young and naive and decided to mail to a regular guest the red lingerie his wife had accidentally left behind in his room.

'You did *what?*' my boss at the time said, clamping his hands to the sides of his head.

'Trust me, his wife will be glad to get it back,' I assured him. 'It's really nice quality lingerie.'

'It may well be – *but it doesn't belong to his wife!*'

'Ohhh . . .'

Now, here I was, working with my husband. He'd thrown in his plumbing career to toil alongside me. We worked hard and promoted and grew the businesses, and managed to save enough to buy a house in Healesville, a lovely little town in the Yarra Valley. Between that mortgage, day-to-day living and his child support payments, every cent counted. And then the impossible happened – in 1994 I fell pregnant, something I'd been told was scientifically and medically out of the question.

I was already five months gone when I found out. My weight constantly fluctuated and I usually only had two to three periods a year so it had been easy to miss. Besides, I was 'infertile' so pregnancy never entered my mind. I didn't feel grown up enough to have a baby. My marriage was a volatile tangled mess, I didn't think my husband would want to have another child, and – most of all – I didn't want to run the slightest risk of growing a boy inside me. His sons had unwittingly governed my life since I first took up with their father and I feared another boy would simply lead to more of the same. I picked a senseless fight in order to tell him I was pregnant later that day, and he was so excited he nearly did a backflip. All of a sudden I thought, 'Maybe this will give me a good life. Maybe this has changed things?' For the first time in my life I started to pray. I begged whatever god was up there to please, please, *please* let me be pregnant with a little girl.

Perhaps because my teenage pregnancy and colossally awful abortion had been heavily loaded with shame and pain I was terrified of the idea of giving birth. I fixated on one antenatal video that showed a glamorous-looking mother puff about three times before her bub came out. 'OK,' I thought, 'I'll have one of those.' I was induced at Albury–Wodonga Hospital and wheeled into the new-age birthing suites. The place had scented candles burning and whale music playing. 'Not on your life!' I told the midwives. 'I want to be in a fully equipped operating theatre!'

At that moment I started to go into labour. 'Do you want an epidural?' a midwife asked.

'Oh God, yes. Just do what you've got to do. I don't want to be part of this.'

The delivery went really badly. It was a country hospital, and the epidural had worn off when they decided they were going to do an emergency Caesarean. It was almost too late but they started cutting into me anyway. All of the

anaesthetic had worn off and 'Arrrggghhh!' It was dia-
bolical. Finally the baby was born naturally. She was a
little girl we named Shannyn. I was so sick and depressed
afterwards that I was almost pissed off when they handed
me a kid who was the spitting image of Bert Newton: big
head, round face, no hair. But quite quickly Shannyn – my
glorious dark-haired beauty – grew to be the spitting image
of me, complete with the wise-cracking attitude and fiery
temperament.

My husband was ecstatic about having a little girl.
He idolised Shannyn from the beginning and he proved
to be a great father who took a hands-on approach while
I slowly recovered from the trauma of her birth. To be fair,
despite the other stuff, he could be a fantastic partner on
his day; he was extremely charming and had a great sense
of humour and – as I had seen with his boys – he was
nothing if not a dedicated parent. He even seemed to step
that up a notch after Shannyn was born. He treasured her.
We treasured her.

The arrival of Shannyn heralded the happiest time I could
remember. During the first twelve months of her life I felt
untouchable. Later we moved to our home in Healesville to
nest. I was a clucky mum who fussed over Shannyn's every
need and I loved every second of it. Bath time, bedtime,
cuddle time, nappy change time, feeding time and lolling-
on-the-bed-staring-smiling-and-laughing-at-each-other time.
Motherhood, it turned out, suited me just fine. I loved the
toys, the little plastic plates and spoons, the tiny nighties
and pyjamas. She was such a strikingly beautiful baby and

toddler that it's hard to believe she started life a kooky, Gold Logie–winning old man.

In 1996 I fell pregnant again only to be gripped by the familiar dread that it might be a boy. I had a scan as soon as I could and almost collapsed with relief and joy when they said it was another little girl. If I'm to be completely honest, had that scan come back the other way, there was every chance I might have had an abortion behind my husband's back. Considering the horror of my teenage abortion, it spoke volumes for my frame of mind relating to the toxic role his sons played in our marriage. Not the boys personally, after all they were just little guys who never chose the situation either. But their presence – whether they were physically with us or not – had huge consequences for me.

The arrival of Sarah – blonde, beautiful, calm and gentle – was as dramatic as a scene from a Jerry Bruckheimer movie. I'd been employed as a bookkeeper for a medium-sized logging firm for a couple of years and I worked until 4pm that day. Half an hour after I got home to Healesville my waters broke. We rang the Mitcham Hospital forty kilometres away in Melbourne but my contractions were already two minutes apart. They told my husband to prepare to deliver the baby on the roadside.

'Not a chance,' I said with a withering look.

We piled into the car and had only made it a few hundred metres down the road when we got stuck behind a traffic accident, with blue and red lights flashing everywhere. When we drew nearer, it looked like the guy who'd crashed his motorbike was quite OK. 'Stop the car!' I shrieked, frantically motioning to my husband to pull over behind the ambulance that was on the scene. 'I'm getting in *there*!' A police officer drove the ambulance while the paramedics sat in the back with me. My husband followed in convoy in our car.

'If we have to deliver en route we'll have to pull over,' one of the paramedics told me. Each suburb we passed through I wondered what location I was going to put on the birth certificate. With sirens wailing and lights flashing, we pulled up at Emergency in Mitcham literally with a minute to spare. Sarah was born sixty seconds later on a gurney in the doorway of the hospital. No drugs. Nothing. Just boom, and there she was. Despite her blockbuster entry to the world, Sarah was an extremely funny, happy little bub who just kind of rolled out of me and said, 'Hiya Mummy!' She was a very pink, very big baby girl. There were a few premature bubs being looked after at Mitcham at the time and they were all in the two- to three-pound (around a kilo) range. Poor little dears. Sarah was nine thundering pounds (four kilos). I'd walk past the premmie babies squeaking like little mice and then I'd hear Sarah bellowing, 'Bring me my milk!'

I said to a nurse, 'I think she might have to ride a bike home!'

From the very start Sarah was strong and resilient in her nature. Pretty soon she would need to be. Both my girls would – more than they could have ever known.

6

THE OTHER KERRY

As the years unfurled, my life would have looked pretty darned good to the outside world. I had two adorable little girls to fuss over, a 'loving husband' and a nicely renovated house in beautiful Healesville. I had a steady job and enough money to make sure my daughters never wanted for anything. They always had front-row seats whenever The Wiggles or Disney on Ice came to town, and I'd even pay for one or two of their little friends to come along. Sometimes I'd go to Target and spend $300 on twenty new outfits for them. I'd stock their rooms with the nicest things I could, from comfy beds and the softest doonas to nice furniture, cuddly toys, beautiful books and fun games to play with.

I didn't mind spending money on myself either – over and above the house renovation, which cost in the vicinity of $50,000 to $60,000. I was never your high-end shopper, though. I never set foot in a Louis Vuitton or Prada store; the likes of Target and KMart were good enough for me. While we lived well we never took overseas holidays (certainly not any more cruises!), nor did we drive prestige cars, own a holiday house, boats, jet-skis or flashy toys – although we did buy a second block of land in a new subdivision in Healesville. I would take friends on holidays to Mildura and pay for everything: accommodation, food, fun – anything – because I was so thankful that they were my friends and I had them in my life. And also, *somehow*, because I could afford it.

Being partial to bling I collected about $20,000 worth of jewellery over the years and I loved buying make-up: it helped paper over the cracks and cover the worry lines caused by the crushing weight of dread. Dressing my life up with baubles and fertilising friendships with cash only served to hide the reality of my marriage and the turbulent, tortured inner-life I led. All of the stuff I bought and the trips and restaurant dinners I paid for barely propped up the flimsy veneer that mine was a good life, a happy life, a successful life. My life was anything but. In the end, no amount of foundation and Revlon lippy could conceal the darkest, ugliest reality of all – that I was a criminal. A really, really bad one.

There is a lot I can't say about the crimes I committed. There are complex and consequential legal reasons that govern what can be revealed about why and how I came to steal my first sum of money via a dodgy cheque, written through the business I was working for, and how it led to a pattern of behaviour that would spiral wildly out of control. I can't even say who else worked there. What I can say is that I honestly doubt anyone suddenly wakes up one day at the age of thirty-four and decides, 'You know what? Today I'm going to start a sideline career as a serial fraudster and risk losing everything and everyone I love in my life.' At least *I* didn't. It started as one mistake at the top of a slippery slope – until I crossed a clear line with the mischievous stroke of a pen for the first time in 1997.

In early 2003, however, I was charged with a fraud that spanned a staggering six years. My criminal arrears had accumulated drip by drip, lie by lie, cheque by cheque: a few hundred here, a few thousand there. Naturally – so as not to get caught – I was constantly attempting to repay the account I was plundering, but gradually I tumbled further and deeper and more hopelessly into the red. Over seventy-two months it all added up to an astronomical amount, and by the time it was all over, the papers reported that it was the biggest white-collar crime committed by a female in the state of Victoria at that time.

I remember the moment the gig was up. I'd been heading to visit friends and family in Mildura and on the way I'd stopped to deposit a forged cheque (worth $3000 or so) at a bank branch in Lilydale, the suburb in Melbourne where we'd tied the knot. The teller looked at the cheque, then looked at me, then looked at the cheque again, and as I walked out of the bank I caught her out of the corner of my eye stepping officiously into a back room. 'You're done for,' a voice in my head announced. 'You're caught.' When I got back from Mildura, the bank manager had informed another person at the company I was working for that the account in question was almost empty.

All I could think to do was call the criminal law specialist Paul Galbally, whose sister-in-law I knew. My reaction was not to call my husband because another thing the outside world had no idea about was how strained things had become with the man who was now my *ex*-husband. Our dysfunctional marriage had been at its worst and was heading for a climactic ending. We both realised this and let animosity take over any reasonable behaviour, as impending divorce often does. Christmas Eve 2000 was the night my marriage ended. It was a done deal in my heart and soul.

So, now that I found myself in serious criminal trouble, I figured Paul would be the right person to represent me. His offices were in the court precinct in the middle of Melbourne and when I sat down at our first meeting I got straight to the point. 'I think I'm going to be arrested for fraud.' There. I said it out loud.

'Right. OK, Kerry, can you tell me exactly how much fraud you think you're going to be arrested for?' Paul responded calmly and politely. At that stage I was under the impression I had slowly siphoned off somewhere in the order of $500,000 – an eye-watering amount in anyone's book. It would almost quadruple by the time I was finally sentenced.

'Maybe half a million dollars.'

'I see. Well if it is $500,000, and you've actually done that, then you're looking at two years in jail.'

I tried to say something but I couldn't speak. I made a feeble coughing noise instead.

'If and when you're arrested,' he continued, 'make sure you ring me immediately.'

'Yes, yes, of course,' I stammered.

The meeting would have lasted forty-five minutes but as I walked back to my car all I could think of was Paul's first sentence at the beginning of our conversation: 'You're looking at two years.' When I climbed inside the car and rang my ex-husband, I blurted out the news: *I'm looking at two years!* With the notion of a prison term sinking in, another sentence swirled inside my skull: 'What about Shannyn and Sarah?'

7

ARRESTED

For three months information filtered back to me via people I knew through the company. Apparently the police were getting ready to bring me in. 'They hate you, Kerry,' I was reliably informed. 'They've got you in their sights and you're going down.' There was nothing I could do but wait. The silence and solitude made it feel as if it was happening to someone else. I sat in front of daytime TV for hours with one eye on the clock, anxious for the next scene to start when the lady with the little girls in the nice house in the pretty town was finally handcuffed and dragged away.

I had no idea the police had me under surveillance. While they were busy getting warrants to search my house, I was busy getting fit. If I was going to prison, I figured I'd need to be as healthy and strong as possible. In between staring at the TV, I hit the gym three times a day for a month.

Once again I felt removed from the process, like I was watching a series about a woman training to get fit so she could face the horrors and rigours of prison. I started off walking on the treadmill and in the end I was running pretty fast and swimming up to thirty laps a day. I was hell-bent on making sure that if prison was my destiny I wasn't going to die in there for lack of preparation.

It was 6am on 8 February 2003 when they finally came for me – at the gym of course. There were five or six officers in all, led by a man with the stock-issue name of Detective Sergeant John Smith. He and his officers bustled into the gymnasium like it was an episode of *Law & Order* and surrounded me while I was sweating it out on the exercise bike. Detective Smith radiated hostility as soon as he walked through the door.

'Kerry Tucker?' he said.

'Yep,' I replied apprehensively.

Without saying a word he moved one hand to his hip and, in the process, brushed his suit jacket aside just enough to reveal the holstered gun on his belt. I was shocked. 'Oh what, really? Are you going to shoot me?' I blurted out incredulously. It sounded like derision and it clearly embarrassed him in front of his junior colleagues, though for once I hadn't intended to be a smart-arse. It was simply that I was Kerry the suburban mum, not Ivan Milat. I wasn't about to go on a killing spree; I was trying to complete a spin class!

From that moment on, Detective Smith cut me absolutely no slack. Although I was hardly a threat to the community,

I would come to understand that I was the biggest story in a small town since the bushfires of 1920-something and everybody wanted a piece of the drama. Out in the car park Detective Smith placed me in handcuffs for everyone to see.

An hour later we pulled up at my house where two police trucks and eight squad cars were parked out the front. I was told the officers belonged to the Purana Task-force – the same outfit that investigated organised crime and gangland killings in Melbourne during the 2000s. The police virtually emptied my house and took everything away, right down to the girls' clothes and toys. Anything that wasn't nailed down was removed, photographed and catalogued. In a welcome relief from Detective Smith, however, the Purana personnel were very nice to me. I was released from the handcuffs and taken inside my home. With 'guests' swarming all over the place I reverted to type. 'Would anyone like a cuppa?' I offered and was greeted with a few enthusiastic nods. I made some coffees and stood in my kitchen while the strangers peered back at me in silence over the rims of their cups.

'Well, this is awkward, isn't it?' I half-joked.

'Not for us. It's our job,' one of the officers said.

'OK, it's a bit awkward for me then,' I replied with a sheepish smile. I fiddled with the cups and spoons at the sink and announced, 'I'm just going to pop off to the toilet. I'll be back in a sec.'

'Not without me you're not!' one of the policewomen said surprisingly forcefully.

'Excuse me?' I responded, rattled.

'You can't go anywhere. You cannot take one step without me.'

At that moment I twigged that my life was about to change in the most profound way. At the gym it had all been a bit surreal but here I was in my own home being told by a person who was sworn to protect the community that I was no longer free – not even to have a wee.

Bzzzzzzzzzzzzzzzzzzzzzzzzzzzz.

When I was led into my bedroom the police had already been through my cupboards and drawers and laid out an array of jewellery on the bed. I was a bit shocked by how much of it I had, to be honest. They started asking me which pieces were real and which pieces were costume jewellery. I was totally truthful and forthright with them; I thought the seasoned officers would be human lie-detectors who'd know straight away if I wasn't being straight with them. I was concentrating on deciphering the value of some fetching earrings when suddenly the bustling room fell silent, apart from one distinct sound.

Bzzzzzzzzzzzzzzzzzzzzzzzzzzzz.

Five or six Purana detectives were standing at the end of the bed taking notes and photographing the ill-gotten jewels when they clearly heard it. A few puzzled looks were exchanged. 'What's that noise?' someone asked, semi-rhetorically. I knew exactly what it was but I wasn't going to say in a million years. I'd heard it as soon as I'd walked in the room. The officer in charge of the search knew, too. When he'd looked through my top drawer he'd obviously stumbled upon my vibrator and accidentally turned it on before hurriedly putting it back. He knew that I knew that he knew – and he could hardly bear to look at me. Well, this certainly *was* awkward – for both of us. Although it was a muffled noise, to my mortified ears it was as loud as a jet taking off.

BZZZZZZZZZZZZZZZZZZ!!!

'Seriously, what the fuck is that noise?!' the Purana detective persisted.

It went on for five minutes. In the end the officer who'd turned it on in the first place could take it no more and fled the room. Then the taskforce detectives put down their cameras and did a snap investigation, scouring the room from top to bottom. I started hyperventilating. I wanted to die. 'Oh, hey look, I've really, *really* gotta go to the toilet if that's OK,' I pleaded. If I didn't get out of the room I was going to have a heart attack. Blessedly my female shadow nodded and I was granted a temporary reprieve from death by humiliation. I sat on the toilet thinking, 'Oh God – just take me to prison now! Please make it stop!' Thankfully, when I re-emerged the vibrator had stopped vibrating. My prayers had been answered. I just hope it was the lady officer who found it.

8

LOCK-UP

At Lilydale police station I was allowed to phone Paul Galbally. Hearing his voice on the other end was an enormous comfort even though his instructions sounded bleak. 'Don't say a word,' he said. 'Whatever the officers ask you, just reply "No comment". Understand?'

'I understand, Paul.'

'OK, good. Now listen, you'll have to apply for bail tonight by yourself. It'll be done when they bring a Bail Justice in to see you.' The courts close at 4pm and it was now well after hours.

'And how do I apply for bail exactly, Paul?' I pressed, a little concerned that he seemed to think I somehow magically knew how to conduct legal proceedings.

'You tell the Bail Justice that you need to remain in the community because you have two small children to care for . . . but,' he added as his voice trailed off a little, 'I don't think you'll get bail.'

More than being fearful I was relieved that Shannyn and Sarah were safe in the care of their father at his place. The prospect of staying in custody overnight wasn't the catastrophe it might otherwise have been. 'OK, no bail,' I said. 'What then?'

'They'll keep you overnight and I'll see you in court in Ringwood in the morning. How are you going really, Kerry? I'm worried about how you're coping.'

By then Detective Smith had returned and was looming over me. I had to shut Paul down quickly because the kindness and concern in his voice were beginning to unravel me. I didn't want to cry – not in front of Detective Smith. 'I'm fine thanks, Paul, really. I'll be alright. I have to go. I'll see you in the morning.'

'OK, Kerry. Remember, "No comment." See you tomorrow.'

I handed the phone to Detective Smith who rang off and announced that he was going to conduct a formal police interview. 'Do you understand?' he asked.

'No comment.'

The Bail Justice arrived around 8.30pm. Detective Smith opposed bail on behalf of the Crown and it was formally refused. For the first time since I was abducted as a teenager I was to be locked up against my will. Only this time there could be no escaping through the bathroom window. There was no room for me at Lilydale so I was driven to the Knox Police Holding Cells just opposite the giant Westfield shopping centre, and signed into the custody of the Watch House officers. As they escorted me along a corridor I heard a voice announce, 'Prisoner coming through!'

'Oh God!' I thought, suddenly alarmed. 'Please don't let me run into any prisoners.' But there was nobody else in the hallway, and it dawned on me that they were referring to me. *I* was the prisoner.

I was passed over to two female officers with about as much ceremony as a dog-catcher drops a stray at a shelter. The women were wearing blue rubber gloves and I doubted they were fixing to do the washing up. I was ordered to step into a holding cell. 'Take your clothes off and hand them to us,' the older officer directed.

'What? All of them?' My head was spinning. I had no idea whether they were even legally allowed to force me to undress or how far they could go.

'Yeah, all of them. Now!'

When the police had come for me I'd been dressed in a matching black Nike top and skirt with runners. Now I stood naked in the middle of the freezing cell while the officers suspiciously picked through my garments looking in vain for drugs or weapons. I thought about how much I had already lost and how much I was continuing to forfeit. And how it was all my fault. I had jettisoned trust and with it friends, my job, my reputation, my liberty, my children, my dignity and now I was being stripped of my sovereign womanhood by two blue-fingered agents of the state. Could it get any worse? Suddenly I became consumed with dread that an internal search was next on the agenda.

'Now open your mouth and show me inside your ears,' the officer continued. I did as I was told. 'Lift up your breasts. Good. Now wiggle your fingers and toes. Right, now turn around slowly. Good, now get dressed.'

I was relieved they didn't do an internal search but I needn't have worried – I later found out it was illegal for the police, Corrections Officers or anyone else to do a physical internal examination of prisoners in Australia. I would also learn what a handy loophole this creates for women to exploit.

Next the officers told me to grab three vinyl cushions and two blankets from a nearby stack and follow them to a 'lock-down' cell. The cushions were just under a metre long and I was instructed to put them on top of a raised concrete slab on one side of the cell – my bed for the night. The blankets were typical army issue, as thick as a Kleenex, itchy to the touch and infused with a dampish aroma that was somewhere between vomit and three-day-old rubbish. There was no pillow. The cell was a tired-looking iron and concrete box with a stainless steel toilet (with no lid), a wash basin, the concrete slab and a seat. The most menacing piece of decor, however, was the security camera mounted in a corner of the ceiling. If I needed to go to the toilet it would be in full view of whichever officers were watching. As luck would have it, I was menstruating.

Outside of being raped I could think of nothing more degrading or intrusive than having to go to the toilet in full view of a crowd of strangers that included men. I fought the urge until my stomach hurt, my bladder stung and blood trickled down my legs. I had to ask an officer for toilet paper and sanitary pads and then sit on the toilet in front of them while I mopped up. It was the most dehumanising, unnatural act I had ever been asked – nay, ordered – to perform.

As I lay down for my first night in a cell, I found that although I was emotionally exhausted I was wired so tight I was unable to switch off. For some reason the man in the cell beside me started screaming and he kept it up all night. Despite it being obvious that I wouldn't be getting any sleep, the officers banged on my cell door every hour to check on my 'emotional state' – though they seemed to think the shrieking maniac beside me was doing just fine.

In the morning Detective Smith returned and drove me to Ringwood police station to await my appearance in the local court. I was stripsearched by more strange women wearing blue rubber gloves before being locked in a holding cell with a young woman named Shannon. I almost burst into tears: she reminded me of my little Shannyn – just with an 'o' and all grown up.

'Do you want a smoke?' she asked. Shannon was casual and at ease as she leaned up against the cell wall, her long blonde hair tied back. I put her at about twenty-five. She spoke in a way that suggested she'd had a good education and I figured she was from a good family. Certainly not the type of girl I expected to find locked in a cell. But then, one could say the same about me, the quintessential suburban mum.

'No thanks,' I demurred, instantly curious as to how she could have got a cigarette into the cell in the first place. The strip-searches were quite thorough. Shannon must have noticed my perplexed expression as she carefully unwrapped the crumpled-looking smoke from a small square of Glad Cling Wrap. 'Hang on, is that a joint?' I asked.

'First time, is it?' she asked in reply. 'It's alright, you can have some. I've got more.'

I was still stumped by how it was possible she had a *joint* on her, let alone access to more marijuana. Then the penny dropped: the Glad Cling Wrap! Shannon didn't have the drugs on her – she had them *in* her. 'Oh no-no-no-no-nooo, but thanks anyway,' I replied, declining her kind offer of illegal drugs fresh from her vagina while locked in the middle of a police cellblock. I couldn't believe it was happening.

As Shannon sparked her BIC lighter – which had been 'banked' in the same place – I went into internal meltdown. In my straight-laced world, drugs were as dangerous as cyanide. I had visions of becoming stoned off Shannon's second-hand smoke, staggering across the road and collapsing in front of the magistrate. I backed away from the young prisoner to the furthest corner of the cell and started taking tiny sips of air like a woman in labour. I was also terrified about what the officers would do if they came in. Shannon wasn't; she might as well have been sitting on a beanbag in her lounge room.

'What are you up for today?' she asked casually as I kept up the weird breathing.

'Bail, I think. Fraud charges,' I said. (Sip-sip-sip . . .)

Once the smoke cleared – and without an officer ever coming near – we spent the next few hours sharing our tales of woe. Shannon, the first heroin addict I had met besides my late cousin Cathy, was facing a string of drug-related charges. She was already on remand at the Dame Phyllis Frost women's prison in Deer Park, which, she assured me, was nothing like what you see in the movies and 'waaaay more comfortable than these cells'. They may well have been, but I didn't want to find out firsthand.

9

HELL HOLE

I didn't get bail. A wave of fear crested and crashed on top of me and I began to say goodbye to my life and my children. If the poor little things could see their mummy now they wouldn't know what to make of it; they'd only cry for me to go home with them. I couldn't bear to think of it – but it was all I could think about. In a room full of busy, officious people, I had never felt so alone. And the day was only just beginning to go downhill.

'The thing in the back is gonna love it at Moorabbin,' the police officer remarked to his partner as we sped down a highway in a divisional or 'divvy' van, with me sliding around in the locked steel box at the rear.

'Who the fuck cares?' his mate scoffed.

The prison at Deer Park was full to capacity so I was to be kept on remand at the Moorabbin Police Holding

Cells until a place became available. Apparently this was good news for me because, I'd been told by an officer at the Ringwood cells, there was an exercise yard at Moorabbin. The divvy van slowed sharply and stopped, sending me thudding into the front of the cage. 'The Thing' had arrived. I was pulled out and marched inside – the last time I'd see daylight for nearly a month.

Straight away I could hear women shrieking and swearing as if a brawl was in full swing. I dared not turn around. 'Dear God, please don't put me in with them,' I prayed. This only brought two female officers wearing the dreaded blue gloves. 'Oh, please no,' I begged them. I still had my period and desperately needed to change my pad. They couldn't care less – the strip show must go on.

I re-dressed and was ordered to get the standard three cushions and two blankets from a stack. As I gathered my 'bedding' I spied four or five women pressed against a Perspex window trying to get a look at their new cellmate – me. A pounding heartbeat or two later I was standing in their midst. As the heavy steel door banged shut behind me I turned to look at it. 'Exercise Yard A' was painted in large yellow letters above it. 'Oh you fool,' I thought. There would be no trees, grass or blue sky – just steel, cement and a salivating wolf-pack of lady criminals. They were onto me within seconds.

'Got any smokes?'

(Not, 'Hello, what's your name? What are you in for?' Or, 'Are you OK?')

'Yes, I do actually.' I was trying to sound amenable and cool. 'A full packet, too.'

The women nearly knocked me over in the rush to be my new best friend. The rapid-fire questions about smokes gave way to heartfelt inquiries about my name, how I was doing and whether they could help me feel more comfortable. I seemed to have transitioned quite well into their ciggie-obsessed world – until they asked exactly when I was going to produce these smokes of mine and when they might get one.

'Oh, I gave them to the officers,' I said, jerking a thumb at the door. 'You can ask them for one.' I presumed that's what the women had done until their cigarettes had run out. How was I to know they'd already been locked up in there – utterly smokeless – for a week or two? When I walked in with talk of a full packet they presumed I'd 'banked' it in the female vault, the same way Shannon had hidden her marijuana. I was promptly labelled a 'fucking green-skin' and abandoned by my new buddies in less than a minute.

Still, one of them was civil enough to direct me to the far cell to put my bedding in. I went back out into the exercise yard and tried to absorb my new, compressed concrete universe. The yard was a rectangular box about fifteen metres by five metres. At one end three concrete stools and a concrete table were cemented into the floor while a concrete bench sat just inside the main door. A security camera was bolted to the roof alongside a fully enclosed television screen.

There was a slot for meals and communication built into the main door. Above the slot was a Perspex window covered by a Venetian blind, so officers could see the prisoners before opening up. The door itself was built into a steel wall with reinforced tinted Perspex at the top so the prisoners could at least see who was arriving at the reception area. It's how the she-wolves had first ogled me.

A door to the left led to a shower that was operated by pushing a button in the wall. Each jab dispensed thirty seconds of water before you had to press it again, with no control over the pressure or temperature. Next to the shower was another steel door leading into a concrete 'visitor's box' – much like the cell I'd just come from at Ringwood.

To the right of the main yard there were three cells about four metres wide by five metres long. This was where prisoners slept, or at least tried to. Each cell had a lidless stainless steel toilet and wash basin with a wall-mounted, stainless steel 'mirror' that only reflected a blurred rendering of any poor soul who dared to look at themselves. There were also two benches; one running the full length of the cell (six cushions) while on the opposite wall there was a standard three-cushion bench. Each cell could accommodate three women on the benches and one, possibly two, on the floor if need be. Cameras in each cell monitored everything. There was a similar cell configuration on the opposite side of the main yard, including a 'drunk tank' for the alcohol-blitzed overnight arrestees, which doubled as a holding cell for everyone else when the officers conducted daily cell and strip-searches. I badly wanted to go home.

When the crushing disappointment about my non-existent cigarettes had abated, the women in the yard grew curious about the fucking green-skin. They lit a conversation, albeit a closely guarded one. At first I was intimidated by their prison banter. I could swear like a sailor but there was a bleak harshness to their profane language. Even so, I soon found them very easy to speak to. It took them thirty seconds to deduce I was a first-timer and drug free – a 'fucking squarehead' in the vernacular.

Kristy and Brooke were both twenty-three-ish and could have passed for sisters. They were athletically built and had long, bottle-blonde hair. Both were also heroin addicts and had young children in the care of family members, which wasn't necessarily a good thing.

Leah was around twenty-five, thin and quiet with a welcoming, friendly smile. Leah was an addict, too, but she seemed to exert control over Kristy and Brooke when they played up. It was obvious they all knew each other on the outside.

Debbie was around my age, approaching forty. She was very quiet and extremely sensitive to just about everything. She, too, was gripped by an addiction to heroin as well as any pills she could get her hands on. Finally, there was Tracey: the most boisterous of the lot. She was in her mid-thirties and clearly an 'old-timer'. Another heroin addict, Tracey was also a good friend of the infamous stand-over-man-cum-self-mutilating maniac Mark 'Chopper' Read. She adored her mum, too; it said so on the tattoo on her arm. And she clearly liked the look of me.

'G'day, goooorgeous!' Tracey cooed as she eyed me up and down. I had never been hit on in quite the same manner in all my years. I couldn't speak. 'What'd they pinch you for, sweetheart?' Tracey continued. My pulse raced and my mouth went dry. For a split second I contemplated telling her I'd committed a horrible murder, but out of nowhere a tiny, nervous voice squeaked the truth.

'Fraud,' the little creature peeped. A couple of seconds later I realised it was me.

'Guessed as much, beautiful,' Tracey breathed. 'Don't worry, we'll look after you.'

That was exactly what I was afraid of.

Once the initial shock of being in Moorabbin morphed into more of a generalised apprehension, I felt strangely drawn to my fellow inmates and soon realised they meant me no harm. Not even Tracey. We were all in the same boat and thus innately shared an intense sense of sisterhood. They were wretched creatures; abused, broken and rough around the edges, but they were unflinchingly honest about who they were. It can't be easy to say, 'G'day! I'm a heroin addict. I will lie, cheat, steal and do just about anything for drugs. That's why I'm in here.' Compared to my crimes – which were committed in comfort, far from danger and neatly covered over by a latticework of lies – these women wore their harrowing stories on their faces, and their hearts on their sleeves. I admired them and felt oddly mesmerised. I suddenly wanted to know everything there was to know about heroin addiction. Maybe if I understood it I could somehow help them?

'Tell me about yourself,' I found myself saying. 'Tell me everything.' So they did. We had a lot of time to kill.

The women revealed some of the biggest hearts and the most soul-destroying histories I had ever heard. They'd all had horrendous childhoods and had staggered along a well-worn path from abuse to the heroin that numbed them just enough to exist. They certainly put my own difficult past into perspective. Where the average woman would likely identify child abuse as the single most damaging event in their lives, to these girls it was a given; their entree to misery. And it only got worse from there. Much, much worse.

I marvelled that these extraordinary people were still capable of any emotion, let alone the empathy they shared and the unconditional support and friendship they quickly offered to me. Maybe it was because I was someone who seemed interested and wasn't going to hurt them, or maybe it was because I was subject to the exact same scorn and disrespect from the police officers who were guarding us. As far as the police were concerned, we were all the scum of the earth.

I was surprised to discover the female officers were the worst. Except for me, all of the prisoners required medication as they were in various stages of withdrawal from opiates. Depending on the officers on duty, medicine was dispensed at whim and not at the same time each day in order to limit the impact of the women 'hanging out' – the painful, searing craving for heroin. Once their bodies started screaming for the drugs they'd become dependent on, the women became agitated, anxious, restless and – with very little provocation – extremely aggressive. It only took me one day in lock-up to realise the officers were playing games with them – just because they could. Welcome to prison.

10

THE SYSTEM

Each day I would open my eyes and be slightly alarmed and then depressed to find I was still in custody. The amount of sleep we got depended on whether anyone had been thrown in the drunk tank overnight. If they had, we were treated to an evening of wall-kicking and screamed obscenities. We were then woken at 7am when the 'cleaner' started blasting the cells, the yard and showers with a fire hose.

About 8am we were each given a towel, a palm-sized rectangle of soap and one compact toothbrush made out of hard rubber and pre-loaded with dried toothpaste. Then breakfast was served. If there were six women in the cells then we got six portions, not a morsel more. The toast had been cooked some days earlier and frozen in pairs inside plastic bags. On the morning of consumption it was microwaved for a minute and handed to us. Mmmm, chewy brown rubber. We were each allowed two motel-sized servings of butter and two of jam but we had to spread it with the back of a plastic spoon since plastic knives were prohibited. Next, lidless plastic containers arrived bearing two Weet-Bix with just enough milk pre-added to ensure they were unappetising. To wash this down we were given one instant coffee in a polystyrene cup – known as a 'brew' in the system. From go to whoa breakfast took around two minutes to consume and two minutes to account for every item supplied.

I, however, refused to eat their heinous fare. Firstly, I had no appetite and, secondly, if that was how I was expected to accept food from another human being then I didn't want it. I had made a conscious and instinctive decision as soon as I was arrested to do everything possible to avoid becoming 'a product of the system'. I didn't want to be tarnished by this place and have it rub off on Shannyn and Sarah when I finally got to see them again. Retaining my sense of self would prove to be one of the very few good decisions I'd made in my life.

My non-breakfast was followed by a shower, but if you weren't showered by the time a passing officer felt you should have been then the towels were taken from you and the showers were locked – just because they could. Years earlier, when I'd been to court during my divorce proceedings, I'd see women being brought into the courtrooms who appeared to have slept in their clothes. Now I know they literally had! After a few days, depending on which officer was on duty, we were sometimes allowed a dollop of shampoo in a plastic cup to share.

After showering, it was up to us to try to wash our own clothes in the wash basin in the cell and then dry them on the damp concrete. Mostly we sat in them wet. Within a couple of days, five out of the six of us had our period and we had to ask a male officer on duty to get us tampons, which he did but – instead of leaving a box in the cells – *he* determined when we should receive them and not a minute earlier. To add creepiness to the humiliation, we had to change tampons in full view of the officers manning the security cameras at the front desk. By 9am the TV was switched on so we would just sit and sit and sit while the girls withdrew from heroin.

As far as the officers were concerned, I was a dream prisoner: drug free, polite and obedient. Yes, I was exerting my iron will when it came to their food, but I didn't ask for anything, complain or take the officers on. Consequently – their deplorable tampon rationing aside – I was treated very well by all of my captors. All except one.

We were entitled to breakfast, morning tea, lunch, after-noon tea and dinner. Morning and afternoon tea consisted of one piece of fruit – either an apple or orange – and coffee. Lunch was exactly the same as dinner; meals served straight from the microwave in plastic containers. Sometimes it was thin slices of vile hamburger meat that had been cooked, then frozen and then microwaved just enough to melt the ice a tad and served alongside two pieces of bread so stale we could snap them in half.

From the day I arrived the lunches and dinners were either not thawed properly or simply off by sight and smell. Bread became our main source of nourishment. In light of this, we relied heavily on the coffee and fruit, and when it wasn't provided tempers flared. I had to keep reminding myself that no one in the cells had even so much as entered a plea before a court. We'd no more been convicted of crimes than the officers guarding us had, yet they treated us like pigs in a pen. Even I was starting to emotionally fray. Something had to give.

We all developed urinary tract infections from holding on too long to avoid peeing in front of a bunch of men. To try to flush our systems we'd rinse the white polystyrene coffee cups and fill them with water from the wash basin to drink throughout the day. Since the cells were searched daily for 'contraband', one female officer, the Tarantula, took it upon herself to remove these cups without fail. It was obvious this woman's greatest pleasure in life was derived from punching downwards. She enjoyed seeing others suffer and go without. One day Kerry the polite and obedient newbie snapped. As the Tarantula swaggered past me with her day's haul of illegal drinking cups, I stared at her and said in a low monotone voice: 'Do you have to work at being a fucking bitch, or does it just come naturally?'

The Tarantula stopped dead in her tracks, took two steps towards me so we were practically butting chins and spoke through gritted teeth: 'That's one smart-arsed comment you are going to regret, *Mizz* Tucker.'

I was by now a far cry from my usual compliant self. Locking someone up indefinitely and stripping them of their dignity will dramatically change them, and I was no exception. 'And what the fuck do you think you can do worse than you're already doing now?' I exploded. 'It's not like I've got a lot more to lose, you fucking cow. Stick your fucking cups up your arse, if there's room up there alongside your shitty fucking personality.'

The Tarantula smiled at me and for a second I thought I'd shown her what for. Wrong! She left me momentarily, pulled on some blue gloves and returned with one of her mates. I was ordered into the single cell and strip-searched before being locked inside alone for four hours. 'You might have some time to re-think how everyone is being treated now, Mizz Tucker,' the Tarantula tut-tutted as she slammed the door shut.

'Third World goats get treated better, you dickhead,' I bellowed back. 'Now fuck off.'

Boy, I sure was getting the hang of the lingo!

Fortunately, not all the officers were arachnids. Two in particular were very kind to me – Sergeant Mill and Officer McInerney. They passed on the messages my family had left and even personally escorted me to a phone so I could call Shannyn and Sarah.

The girls whispered into the phone almost as if they felt loud voices might hurt me. 'Mummy, please come home tonight,' Shannyn sobbed. Her words were wrapped in sorrow and heartbreak. 'Sweetheart, I can't come home tonight but I will see you very soon,' I replied. 'Just remember, Mummy loves you, wherever I am.' Sarah heard my voice and just cried; she couldn't squeeze one word between her sobs. I knew I was sinking fast and started to tell her I had to go. She screamed, 'Don't go, Mummy!' And with that I told her I loved her, to be strong and I'd call again very soon. And then they were gone.

I'd return to the yard after these painful contacts with my girls desperately upset. To my initial surprise, all of the women rallied around to make sure I was OK and tried to lift my spirits off the cold concrete floor. As they became more protective of me I became more and more fascinated by them. They possessed a capacity for kindness and empathy in the face of calamity that I had not thought possible.

I had never given prisoners much thought. Why would I? My life had played out a world away from theirs. Once upon a time I might have abstractly dismissed them as junky scum like everybody else, but now that I was on bread and water with them I saw heroic survivors of unspeakable degradation. No matter how strong their bonds or how resilient they seemed to the relentless tide of violence, fear and dysfunction in their lives, they were ultimately helpless against the judicial and 'correctional' machine.

The crushing weight of the system can squash a person flat, emotionally and physically. Take me – in my first ten days in custody I lost 6.5 kilos, and as I gazed at ravaged faces around me I wondered how I was going to look after two years.

The average time spent on remand in the cells was usually around two days. But the five women who'd welcomed me had already been there a week when I arrived, with no prospect of being moved any time soon. In the meantime the Moorabbin cells continued to fill up with traumatised women, delivered daily by the conveyor belt of justice.

Tracey possessed a ferocious temper. She was on remand in the wake of a vicious road-rage encounter. Another driver had bumped into her car, but when the parties pulled over to inspect the damage Tracey attacked the three people who'd climbed out of the other car with a baseball bat and nearly crippled them. As more and more women were added to the cells, fuses like Tracey's grew shorter. Meals were now being delivered completely frozen or totally off. You could just smell it. The meat was rancid and, in some meals, too hot on the outside and bleeding or frozen in the middle. This triggered a pathetic cycle of women yelling at officers, officers ignoring women, women kicking walls, officers yelling at women, meals being taken away and put in the rubbish, and women going hungry.

Finally, the food got so bad we could no longer accept it. We were contending with an outbreak of diarrhoea as well as head lice, hunger, extreme cold and sleep deprivation. I began to fear that an uprising might erupt, but something unexpected happened instead.

One morning, Brooke requested a pen and paper to write to the Ombudsman. 'Now there's an idea,' I thought. As I listened to how this letter was to be addressed to 'The fucking Ombudsman re. these dog bastards in this shit hole', I saw an opportunity to help. 'Why don't you let me write the letter for you?' I suggested. 'I used to write official letters all the time.'

'Yeah, well go on then, but you let 'em know that we're fucken pissed off, alright?' Brook instructed.

'Of course.'

Soon the other women huddled around the little concrete table in the yard that had become my office as I prepared to write. 'Make sure it goes to the head arse-hole,' commanded Tracey, now taking ownership of the correspondence.

'Yep, you talk, I'll write,' I said.

'OK,' she began, 'well . . . "To the fucken head honcho at the fucken Commissioner's place." I want it to go straight to the fucken top!'

I dutifully took her dictation: *For the Attention of the Ombudsman.*

'Tell the fuckers it's about the fucken shit food these rats serve up in this fucken cunt of a place.'

I put pen to paper again. *Re: Human rights, hygiene and nutrition concerns at the Moorabbin Holding Cells.*

'Tell 'em we're fucken pissed off and if I get hold of one of these rat dog cunts I'll kill the motherfucker.'

We have genuine concerns that are contributing to aggressive behaviour, and our relationship with the officers is becoming increasingly strained. The officers are providing us with food that is unfit for human consumption.

'Tell 'em I'll shove any more shit food squarely up their fat, dog arses!'

It appears that we are now in a situation where we must decline to accept such food and we shall return it to the officers.

'Tell 'em, if they don't do something we'll fucken riot. We'll take the fucken lid off this fucken tin can!' Tracey was pretty much yelling now while the others mumbled their agreement with her oration.

'OK, got that,' I said eagerly.

We are currently working on conflict resolution opportunities but the possibilities are restricted.

'And if these dogs don't get back to us soon, I'll fucken kill them too!'

We would appreciate an early response to our concerns to avoid the likeliness of further conflict.

'Tell 'em they'd wanna fucken listen, right? Ya got that?'

Thank you for your consideration and attention to this matter.

'Fucken maggots,' Tracey signed off with a dismissive wave of her hand.

Yours sincerely,
Inmates at Moorabbin Cells

'Now send the fucker,' she said, stamping her foot like some sort of Gestapo salute.

The girls were so excited and outwardly impressed by my wordiness that I figured this was probably the first iota of support anyone had given them in a long time. I had no idea this rather rudimentary letter would set me on a course that would have a massive impact on the rest of my life.

First, though, we were faced with a new problem: getting it to the Ombudsman. Our best bet was Sergeant Mill, a compassionate and helpful officer, but to get to him we had to go through the Tarantula. As expected, she mocked us before passing the letter on to an equally nasty woman from the CIB Division who waved it in front of us. 'The Ombudsman will never get it,' she vowed.

Every moment of empowerment the girls had just enjoyed was ripped from them and rubbed in their faces. So it was a very pleasant surprise when Sergeant Mill advised us a few hours later that he had retrieved the letter and faxed it through to the Office of the Ombudsman for us. We were elated.

When the Ombudsman arrived a few days later, the officers stood at attention and pretended to be on chatty terms with us before we were individually interviewed. I was the last to go in and the Ombudsman knew immediately I was the one who'd written the letter. I told her our complaints were most definitely justified and went into minute details about the officers' mind-games, the rancid food, the appalling hygiene and the egregious and needless deprivation of our most basic rights. I took particular care to catalogue the Tarantula's cruel and punitive approach to her job. The Tarantula stood behind the Ombudsman and glared daggers at me in a vain attempt at intimidation. I figured she couldn't do much more to upset us. (Oh, how wrong I was!) The Ombudsman promised to address the issues and wished me well on my journey through the system. Then she left me with the Tarantula.

11

NO BAIL, THANKS

In addition to sporadic phone calls with my girls and their father, I was kept up to date with life on the outside world via visits from my younger brother and a couple of sisters. Most of the family had been present at a meeting held at Paul Galbally's office. Paul told them the likelihood of my getting bail was 50/50, given the serious nature of the charges. The amount I was alleged to have stolen had been steadily climbing and was fast approaching $1.5 million.

Not only that, police were seeking strict conditions, if bail were granted at all. These included that I be bailed to someone else's home – namely my ex-husband's, or my brother's and his wife. Even though that would have allowed me to leave the Moorabbin hell hole and be with my girls while I awaited trial, I simply could not and would not entertain the thought of either option.

I'd had plenty of time in the cells to contemplate my future, and my past. No matter how tangled and twisted the circumstances of my offending, the fact remains I knowingly committed crimes. I *did* steal money – a lot of it – and I knew all along it was bad. 'Thou Shalt Not Steal.' It was wrong when I was a little girl grasping for something to be forgiven for and it was wrong now when I actually had something for the confessional. I easily made up my mind to own up fully to what I had done and to accept any punishment on the chin. It was the only honourable thing to do. I would plead guilty.

Strangely, I was finding my feet in prison – the last place I would have expected. I might have been trapped but I wasn't the pinball anymore. Although I was being ground down by the heel of the system I found myself standing taller than I had in a long time. I knew I could grab onto this place and survive it. Through sheer dint of their continued existence the women I was condemned alongside showed me it *was* possible to survive. If they could, I sure as hell could. I instructed Paul Galbally not to apply for bail. If I was going to be forced to leave my little girls for two years I'd rather start the process now than simply delay it. Hopefully by the time I was released not too much damage would have been done and I could start to rebuild my life with them.

'Are you absolutely certain, Kerry?' Paul pressed me over the phone.

'Yep, one hundred per cent,' I said. 'Lock me up. I'm going in. I'm happy to go to prison and get this thing happening right now.'

Around this time Tash arrived in the cells. She was six months' pregnant and a diagnosed schizophrenic with bipolar disorder. She was in for shoplifting (to support her 'man's' heroin habit) and she almost immediately became psychotic. Seeing her shift quickly through agitation, aggression to rage and near hysteria defied belief. It was terrifying to behold. When Tash was 'normal' she was a caring and gentle soul who couldn't understand why people treated her the way they did. She was also well aware of her condition and would often beg us to silence the voices between her ears. Phantoms from inside the TV insulted her or challenged her judgements and made barbed remarks only Tash could hear. When she started to lose it her face would contort so much she looked like a different person altogether. That scared the pants off me.

Thankfully Tash usually sat quietly, patting her belly and hoping her baby would be a girl, a feeling I knew well. She was going to name her Chilli. Tash already had two boys who'd been split up and fostered out. Her man, Brian, was nothing short of the Son of Sam and had ripped out most of her hair with his bare hands, or what was left of it anyway after he'd set it on fire. He had beaten Tash sense-less every other day and was one of the main reasons her children would not be returned to her. She'd spent the week locked in police cells after being sentenced to two months' prison. She was then transferred to us. Within minutes we knew we were dealing with someone who shouldn't be in prison; she should have been in a secure psychiatric unit.

Who'd have thought I'd end up getting a look inside one of these myself?

12

THE BIGGER SYSTEM

After yet another one of our verbal showdowns – this one over her refusal to give fifteen festering women a single squirt of shampoo – the Tarantula decided to extend my punishment to everyone else in the cells. With my final insult still hanging in the air, she stormed off and returned with a clutch of officers wearing their blue rubber gloves. They herded us into the drunk tank while our cells were turned over, then each woman was pulled out of the tank and forcibly strip-searched. But try as she might, the Tarantula could not break my spirit. There was only one way to cripple me and I had to be careful not to think about it too much. Or think about them, as it were.

Like every mother, my children are a fundamental part of me. They are the embodiment of my very heart; more important than the sun and the air. I would gladly die for them if I had to. Shannyn, my sparky little 'Mini-Me', was seven and Sarah the cuddly, dreamy blonde was just five when I was marched out of our home. By leaving them I was now hurting them. I don't have the words to express the agony this realisation inflicted on me, particularly knowing I was powerless to stop it. If I thought about my girls too much or too deeply I felt myself start to unravel to a point where I might start to cry and never, ever stop. Some days it was relatively easy to distract myself with the present task of surviving in lock-up. Other days, not so much – particularly if I knew it was raining.

We couldn't see, hear or smell the outside world from inside our hollowed-out brick. One evening I heard an officer remark that it was raining and I badly wanted to go out and stand in it, tilt my head to the heavens and feel the droplets kiss my face and wash away the grime and shame. In the next moment I became grief-stricken and panicked. Shannyn and Sarah would always run to me during a storm. I'd scoop them into my lap and coo that they were safe with Mamma. When it stormed I'd hug them tight and show them how to count the seconds between the lightning and thunder so they knew when it was moving away. 'What if they're frightened now?' I shrieked inside my head. 'They need me!' I convulsed in spasms of sobbing that I thought might last forever. I knew then I had to put all of those memories into a little box, close the lid tight and store it deep within me. 'Open at Own Risk.'

Unlike most of the mothers alongside me, I was blessed that my babies were in the care of an excellent father.

However I felt about how he'd treated me, I knew with certainty that he cherished our girls and would always try to protect them from harm. On one level I was enormously sad for him; I knew the heartbreak he'd see in their eyes every day – I heard it each time their little voices pleaded down the phone. 'Mamma, please come home. *Please!*' He was the one who had to explain that Mamma simply was not coming home. Not tomorrow. Not next week. Not for years.

The only thing I knew for sure was that I wanted my daughters back. To do that I would have to fight hard. They would have to be my pot of gold at the end of the rainbow. No matter how far into the future that rainbow arced, they would be on the other side of the prison walls when I walked out. I chose not to add my tears to the rain. I chose to battle instead. The first step would be bringing the girls to visit so they could see me and I could start to explain why Mamma had to stay in the prison. There was no way I was going to have them brought to the Moorabbin Hilton for fear of scarring them forever. We agreed that their father would bring them after I'd been transferred to Deer Park. The days would pass quickly enough.

In the dead of night a woman was thrown in the tank for minor drunk and disorderly charges. But she was no ordinary tipsy girl. She was known to some of the inmates in the cells opposite ours as being from a major Melbourne crime family. She was blind drunk, withdrawing and clearly pissed off at being incarcerated. Her furious objections set the other women off, which only sent Miss Crime Family into hysterics. Unwisely, she attempted to intimidate the girls by bragging about her underworld connections and to 'square up' against them. I could hear the girls on the other side trying to work out her identity through a process of deduction. They also knew the crime families and had close and personal associations with various members of the one cited by our new guest. They weren't at all intimidated. Finally, one figured out who she was and the psychological torture commenced. It didn't take long for the girl in the drunk tank to go quiet as the women mercilessly taunted her. After a while everyone went quiet. You could hear a pin drop.

In the next instant there was an explosion of noise. The watch-house door was almost torn off its hinges as a stampede of boots thundered into the cellblock. We could hear their panicked exchanges. The girl had stripped naked and was in the process of hanging herself. They managed to get to her in time. Instead of calling for an ambulance, they simply removed her clothes from the cell and left her there naked. After all, she was breathing! She was silent and no longer a threat to herself! What more could you want? It was all sorted in under ten minutes. On the way back out one of the officers commented that it was raining outside. I rolled over on my vinyl mats and tried not to think about my girls.

The days ahead brought only more chaos. One after-noon a very large, very powerful woman named Kath was brought in. Apparently, as soon as she'd arrived in a divvy van, she'd tried to fight every officer at reception. So, of course, they quickly threw her in with us. Kath wanted out – now – and she figured the best way forward was to take one of the girls hostage. Kristy was the unlucky one in closest reach. Kath wrapped one of her massive arms around her neck and threatened to break it as she dragged her to a back corner of the yard like a lion with prey. Five officers burst in and tore Kath off Kristy, placed her in a vice-like headlock and hauled her into an isolation cell. By now a pale shade of blue, Kristy slumped to the floor and lay there dazed and unattended by the officers.

That incident was just par for the course in the cells, so I was more than a little relieved when – twenty-four days after I was first thrown into that dank, freezing cellar – the time came for my transfer to the women's prison at Deer Park, or the Dame Phyllis Frost Centre (DPFC) as it is now known. It housed around 300 women and was adjacent to the men's maximum-security Port Phillip Prison.

A few of us who'd been at Moorabbin the longest were going over as a group. I couldn't believe I'd soon see the sky again; maybe even feel sun on my skin or wind in my hair. Most of all, I was excited, though also somewhat daunted, by the prospect of seeing Shannyn and Sarah. Hopefully they'd still recognise me – I'd shed almost ten kilos in three-and-a-half weeks.

We were marched from the yard to an enclosed garage where the Brawler was waiting. It was the biggest steel cattle truck I had ever seen; a fearsome-looking beast that would have been right at home on the set of a *Mad Max* film. This lumbering prison on wheels contained separate enclosures for women and men, and even had solitary cages for troublesome prisoners. There were no lights, no windows and no ventilation. I wouldn't be seeing the sky after all – just suffocating pitch blackness.

Three claustrophobic hours later – after dropping off and picking up prisoners from various courts – it became obvious that the Brawler had left the city. The driving became erratic and very, very fast. With no seatbelts to tether us to the steel benches, we were all thrown about like rag dolls. One woman was knocked out cold. It was obvious that as far as the driver was concerned he might as well have been carting garbage to the tip. Finally the Brawler slowed and the gates rolled up at the DPFC. Only then did it finally sink in that I was no longer in the wretched Moorabbin Police Holding Cells. That part of the nightmare was over. In a few days I'd be seeing my babies. With that to look forward to I started to feel a little like my old self again.

It was 2.30pm on Wednesday, 11 June 2003 when the door of the Brawler swung open and emptied me into a new chapter in my life. As I stepped down into the open I was assailed by sunshine and the smell of grass. I could have cried with gratitude but the moment was short-lived. 'This way, ladies,' a woman said, and led us to the reception building where we were promptly locked in a three metre by three metre holding cell. It was immediately apparent that this place was the real deal.

The first thing I noticed was the demeanour of the officers. These were Corrections Officers, not police. For one thing, Corrections Officers smiled and didn't seem to yell. They were also ranked according to the little dots on the shoulders of their uniforms rather than stripes. They didn't carry guns and they generally seemed less threatening – to me, anyway. Not so the other girls; they'd all been here before and knew the drill. I peered out the cell window and across a concrete quadrangle – 'the compound' – to catch my first glimpse of the razor wire that ringed the entire complex. I'd only ever seen the stuff in movies and now it stood ominously between me and my liberty.

If Paul Galbally was right, I would be here for the next two years.

13

INSANE

One by one the other girls were taken from the cell and led away to be processed. After three hours it was my turn. I was taken into a small office by a pleasant female officer who promptly took my photograph. She didn't ask me to smile. I was given a towel from a washing basket on the floor that had my name on it, plus some blue tracksuit pants, a windcheater, bra, socks and a pair of prison-issue runners. Then I was directed to a screenless shower. Once naked, I was handed a lice treatment that smelled like rocket fuel and told to douse myself in it head-to-toe. Another female officer watched my every move but, given the monumental number of strip-searches I'd endured at the hands of the Tarantula, I was an old hand at public nudity.

Clean, deloused and dressed I was led to another office and interviewed. 'How are you going, Kerry? Can I call you Kerry?' the officer began, and pushed a packet of cigarettes and a lighter across the table towards me.

'Yes you can and I'm doing OK, thanks.'

Over the next hour she took down administrative details including my next of kin, children, barrister's details and medical history. 'Well then, Kerry, the only other thing we need to talk about is protection. Do you need any?' she asked. I was thinking sanitary pads but the officer noticed my confusion and saved me the embarrassment of asking for clarification. 'Protection is a secure area for women coming in for crimes against children, or who are testifying against a co-offender, or who have major issues with any women already in prison,' she said, before adding reassuringly, 'I think you'll be just fine.'

She closed the folder and looked at me earnestly. 'OK, Kerry, a couple of bits of advice. Firstly, and most importantly, trust no one. Secondly, keep your cigarettes out of view of other women as they're like currency on the compound. Most new girls are stood over for their cigarettes and usually just give them up to avoid the confrontation. I hope this doesn't happen to you.'

'Me too.'

'And thirdly, Kerry,' she continued, 'trust no one.'

'Trust no one. Got it.'

I was taken to an adjacent room and told to get naked again. I was about to find out that when doing stripsearches, Corrections Officers go the extra mile to try to stop any contraband slipping through their blue fingers and into the prison. Consequently they looked for drugs and weapons in my mouth, ears, nose, hair, on the soles of my feet, in between my fingers and toes and under my breasts. 'OK, turn around and face the wall.' I did as instructed. 'Good, now bend over and hold each cheek with your hands, and pull them apart.'

Awful scenarios tore through my mind. 'Are they going to do an internal search? I'm not prepared for this!' I figured if anyone knew about the secret business of a woman's internal bank it would be seasoned prison officers, and I reckoned they might just have the authority to go 'in there'. But, much to my relief, no such invasion was launched.

I re-dressed and was taken for a medical. The doctor seemed pleased to see an inmate who was 100 per cent drug free and in excellent physical health. Next I met with a Corrections psychiatrist. 'So, you're here now?' he said, not so much a question as a useless statement of fact.

'It appears so,' I replied.

'Are you feeling suicidal?'

'No, not yet.'

'Have you ever attempted suicide in the past?'

'No.'

'No self-harm? Wrists? Something like that?'

'No!'

By now a couple of the women from Moorabbin had been taken into the Remand Unit, known as A5, but there were no beds available for the rest of us. Kristy was going to stay in the medical division while Deb and I were to be taken to another unit. We picked up our washing baskets and were escorted into the freezing blackness of the night.

Once inside our destination building, A6, we entered a long corridor with six large steel doors on either side: the cells. Before I was locked up, I was allowed to take a call from one of my sisters, Cheryl, at the front desk. She was anxious to tell me that Shannyn and Sarah would be coming to see me on Sunday, in just four sleeps.

'Are you alright?' Cheryl asked urgently. 'We're so worried about you.'

'I'm fine, honestly I am. Please don't worry so much. You know I'll be OK. I've just arrived so I can't tell you that much. I'm only concerned about the girls.'

'Will you be able to ring them tomorrow?' she asked.

'Surely,' I said, but I honestly had no idea.

Shannon with an 'o' from Ringwood cells had been right. The cells at Dame Phyllis Frost were *waaaay* better. I was put into a disabled cell – twice the size of a regular one. And it was warm! Tonight I would sleep between sheets on a mattress. I even had a pillow and a doona. I could use the shower when I wanted and I was armed with sachets of shampoo, conditioner and a comb. After I scrubbed the de-lousing pesticide from my hair and skin and replaced the toxic fumes with the reassuring scent of Palmolive, I climbed into the bed thinking of Shannyn and Sarah. 'I'll see you soon, darlings,' I whispered into the darkness. That night I dreamed about giving birth to them and being happy.

'Stand by your door for muster.' The command blasted over the prison PA system at 7.45am. Muster was a count of every single inmate in the prison to ensure no one had escaped. It happened four times a day, every day. The first was in preparation for the en-masse release of prisoners from their cells at 8am, heralded by the command, 'Movements may commence.' When the officers unlocked my cell door, however, I didn't move an inch. After ten minutes frozen to the spot, I finally worked up enough nerve to nudge it open a millimetre, and then another. Suddenly I got some help – the door was yanked wide open by possibly the largest woman I had ever seen. She filled the entire doorway as she nonchalantly stuffed half a sandwich into her massive mouth using fingers the size of hotdogs. Despite her alarming size and presence, I could see she had friendly eyes. She introduced herself as Robyn.

'Oh, hi. I'm Kerry,' I said nervously.

'Come outside and have a smoke. I'll introduce you to the girls,' Robyn mumbled through a mouthful of bread. 'Follow me. It'll be the best thing for you, being new and all.'

Looking past her into the corridor I was reminded of the final scene in the film *Who Framed Roger Rabbit* when the brick wall around Toon Town is knocked down to reveal the chaos within: marching bands and crazy cartoon characters running about in every direction. It was obvious these were no ordinary women. I was spellbound and horrified at once. 'Holy shit. Am I in a psychiatric unit?' I wondered. Robyn handed me a cigarette and pulled me into an enclosed outdoor yard where two obese women – both dressed the same as me – were hunkered down at a table. 'Kerry, this is Bomber,' Robyn said, gesturing to the one who was sucking on a Red Skin.

'What's doin' and all that?' Bomber said, holding up her hand as if to high-five me.

'Nice to meet you, Bomber,' I said, opting for a toothy smile instead of a sticky hand slap.

'And over here, Kerry, we have Sparky,' said Robyn, turning to another woman in her forties with faded tattoos on her arms. 'Sparky, meet Kerry.'

'Gidday there! Welcome to the nut house,' Sparky slurred.

'Oh, hello. Thanks!' I said brightly, although my internal voice urgently whispered, 'You're in the nut house. You're in the nut house. You're in the nut house . . .'

Robyn took me aside for a background briefing. 'Now listen, Kerry. I thought I'd let you know that the girls here are really great, but some are real fucking head cases. Bomber threatens to blow up airports, judges, the prison – things like that. And Sparky, well Sparky likes to set fires. Big motherfucker fires.'

'Oh, OK then,' I said, bereft of what to say.

Robyn had issues too; borderline personality disorder, apparently, but I couldn't see anything borderline about it – her affliction was full-on. One minute she was light-hearted and funny and the next she'd explode with rage. I was walking alongside her later in the morning when she tried to get the attention of an officer and was either not heard or ignored. In a flash Robyn picked up a plastic chair and hurled it against a wall with such force one of the legs snapped off. That got the officers' attention; it took five of them to restrain her and one to cinch the handcuffs around her giant Christmas-ham wrists. They threw Robyn into her cell screaming blue murder all the way.

While Robyn was locked down, the officers helped me fill out my visitor and telephone contacts lists. I was told I could have ten visitors on my list at any time. Each person was the subject of a police check and also had to be approved by the prison. If they weren't on the list, they didn't get in. Same with the phone list: ten people could be programmed into the system once they'd been approved by the prison. To make a call, inmates had to lift the receiver of one of the phones stationed around the prison, enter their ID number and a four-digit pin code and then select a phone number from their list of ten. Every call was limited to twelve minutes, then the phone cut out. They were also monitored and taped.

Since my phone numbers were yet to be put into the system, an officer allowed me to ring my girls from the office. With my heart in my mouth, I dialled the number and Shannyn immediately picked up.

'Hello sweetheart, it's Mummy!'

'Hi Mummy! Can we come and see you on Sunday?' Shannyn squeaked excitedly, definitely happier than our last call.

'You bet you can, sweetie. I can't wait. I'm counting the sleeps until then. Are you OK, Shannyn?'

'Yes, but I'm still really sad.' Her voice was dropping.

'So am I, sweetie. So am I. But it makes me really happy that I'll be seeing you very soon.'

'Me too, Mummy . . . um . . . Mummy, I cried last night because I missed you. So did Sarah.'

'Sweetheart, it's OK to cry,' I said, trying to soothe her. 'When you feel like crying just remember how much I love you and try to think that it's only three more sleeps until we see each other. Then we'll have lots of kisses and cuddles, OK?'

'OK, Mummy, I love you. Daddy wants to talk.'

The girls' father told me Sarah was in the bath but I could talk to her tomorrow. 'She's fine,' he said. 'They're both a lot better now. I'll bring them in on Sunday morning and they can stay for the afternoon visit as well.'

'Thank you,' I said. Then the line went dead. Twelve minutes flies when you're dying inside.

14

REMAND

It came as a relief when an officer told me that while, yes, I was indeed in the prison's unit for the criminally insane, I was only staying until a bed became available in the A5 Remand Unit. The next morning I was paged to the office and told a 'peer educator' was waiting for me outside. Andrea had been in Dame Phyllis Frost for a while and it was now her job to help all new inmates learn the rules of the compound – 'crim style'. Even Corrections recognised there was a code of conduct in prison and first-timers needed to learn it – primarily for their own safety. Andrea and four other prisoners had been trained especially to do so. It was a respected and privileged job: peer educators were the only inmates allowed access to all of the units, including Management (Isolation) and the Protection Unit.

Andrea was an attractive woman in her forties with a thick mane of red hair and a warm smile she brought to life with blood-red lipstick. I liked her straight away. She was German and spoke in a mishmash of abrupt guttural tones and English. She got straight down to brass tacks. 'The most important thing you need to know in here is not to talk to the officers about anyone, OK?' she said. 'See no evil, hear no evil, speak no evil.'

'Yes, of course. No evil at all. Thanks.' Obviously the horse had already bolted on 'Do no evil'.

Andrea had been in Australia for eight years and three months – half of it in prison – and she still had eighteen months left to serve for her part in a high-profile cocaine importation ring. We spoke for an hour to get acquainted before she left me, with the promise of catching up soon. Later in the day I was ordered to grab my basket and make my way across to the main prison compound – a large open area with concrete walkways snaking off to the leisure centre, administration building and education and program buildings – to the A5 Unit, which looked like a prison within a prison. Waiting to greet me was an officer straight out of Central Casting. Miss Johnson was in her fifties, with a stocky build and a face that had seen many a hard year working in prisons. Her thick Scottish brogue took some getting used to. 'Now, you haven't got to worry about all the things you gave a fuck about before, when you've got a bed here,' she said, fixing me with a flinty stare. 'You've just got one thing to worry about now. Me!'

The Remand Unit was much older and shabbier than the A6 Psychiatric Unit and was not unlike a domed army barracks, only with a large fish-bowl office in the middle and twenty-six cells on either side – room for fifty-two inmates in all. I was directed to 'A Side', where all new arrivals were held for observation purposes. 'B Side' was for the women who'd been incarcerated a bit longer and had settled in. Adjacent to the cells was a kitchen and common area with a few lounge chairs strewn about and a TV sitting on top of a table. My new cell was half as big as the roomy, heated disabled cell in A6, but I counted my blessings that I wasn't crippled or criminally insane.

If I stood in the middle of the cell and stretched my arms I could almost touch the walls on either side. There was a concrete bed and desk on one side and a toilet, shower and shelving on the other. The only things not bolted down were a tiny television on the shelving and a jug on the desk. A little Perspex window with a ventilation grate running down the side provided a view to the glistening razor wire that sprouted from the hard, flat plains of Deer Park like a steel tree line. While most people were in Remand for about two months before they were transferred to the long-term B and C Units, I'd still be in that cell a year later.

You could have cut the tension in A5 with a knife, not that the women could be trusted with one. In A6 the inmates had been confused and vulnerable; in Remand they were hostile and ruthless. Most had been locked up before and weren't happy about being back. The 'A Side' was a particular hotbed of emotions as the women battled to establish themselves in the pecking order. Together they formed a who's who of criminal offending, from prostitutes, burglars, thieves and drug smugglers to women charged with serious assault, arson and murder. Walking among them felt like tiptoeing through a mine field; one wrong step and . . . well, I shuddered to think.

Soon enough a woman named Gail – an apparently notorious criminal with underworld connections – decided I'd make a good target. 'Give us a smoke,' she demanded without the slightest regard for good manners. I may have looked like a little pushover but I was learning fast and the past month had hardened me. I'd had my children taken off me so I had nothing else to lose. The next step down, as far as I was concerned, was death. 'No,' I said staring up at Gail who was, quite literally, standing over me. 'I'm pretty keen to hang onto them at the moment.'

'Right, come outside,' she demanded.

'Nah, I'm pretty good in here,' I said.

'You're coming outside and that's fucking that!'

I could sense ears pricking up around the unit as the old-school crim clashed with the stubborn little newbie. 'Do you know what?' I said, getting to my feet, 'I've been belted by people a good four inches taller than you. I've just lost my kids. I've got nothing else to do so I'll go outside, no problem. I've never been in a fight before and you're going to win this – but you're sure as shit going to know you've been in a fucking fight.' I'd heard this line in a movie and felt that now might be the perfect time to recite it.

Now everyone in the unit was interested. Gail had just been called out but, apparently clean out of ideas and bravado, she let it slide. 'You're fucking crazy,' she spat. 'I'm steering clear of you.' As she walked away I heaved a huge sigh of relief. I learned later she was one of the old-school prison crew and fancied herself as somewhat of a heavy. Regardless, no one had ever taken her on until that day. It gave me an inkling that I might just be able to negotiate the place using my mouth. I had a gift for the quick retort and these were street girls who had a very limited vocabulary. As time went on, and when they were on the receiving end of a verbal volley from me, they mostly ended up retreating. In my case, the mouth was definitely mightier than the muscle.

In the DPFC hierarchy, Remand inmates were the lowest, and even then those on B Side demanded respect from the new women on A Side. I heard a group of B-Siders discussing my credentials as they hunkered down around the TV. 'The new girl? Nah, no big deal. A clean-skin – total square-head. First time. White collar. She's nothin'.' In just over a month I'd gone from being a 'mummy' – a near deity at the centre of not one but two universes – to the lowest scum in Australia; so worthless that maximum-security prisoners held me in contempt. It occurred to me that I could at least fall no further. This was rock bottom and the only way back to my girls was up. I had to start climbing, pronto.

I dedicated the following days to getting to know every woman on A Side. It quickly became clear I was the healthiest person among them. Most of the girls were hanging out and as sick as I'd seen anyone. Following my heart and my gut instinct I started to help them. At first all I could do was sit and listen, but after a while I cottoned on to the prison trade system so I could at least scrounge extra cordial and sugar for them. Mostly, though, I just wiped their brows and listened to their stories. It became a demanding full-time job surprisingly quickly.

In turn the women realised I didn't care what they were, only about what they were going through. They were used to being judged and spat upon, and they definitely expected it from squareheads; people who could never understand or empathise with addicts. For some reason, I did – unconditionally. I felt for them so much it would bring tears to my eyes and I became extremely protective of them. How could one not feel for the girls who couldn't crawl out of their cells on their own? The girls who had no one to care whether they lived or died? The girls the officers ignored?

The perception of non drug users in prison is not a good one. If anyone is going to give up women with drugs it will be a squarehead because they have no vested interest in protecting the trafficking system. I couldn't have cared less – what they did was none of my business and I told them so. Before long I had the women's confidence and trust.

In Remand there's a tendency for the sick, loud and in-your-face women to cast a cloak of invisibility over the frightened and quiet ones. I was frightened but I wasn't quiet, not like Sharon. Another first-timer, she was even shorter than me, a bit dumpy and as quiet as a church mouse. A white-collar 'fraudy' like me, Sharon was outwardly terrified and had made no friends, preferring the semi-solitude of her cell. One night, in between bursts of anguished screaming from the wretched heroin girls, I heard her weeping. I decided to befriend her the next day.

I hadn't seen Sharon since morning muster and as the clock ticked down to the 11.45am count she was still nowhere to be seen. I went to her cell, gently knocked on the door and pushed it open a little. Sharon seemed to be fast asleep but as I bent over her bed I saw a sickening puddle of gore soaked into the doona beneath her ghostly white body. As my mind adjusted to the lurid scene I realised there was blood everywhere; on Sharon, under her, beside her and running in sticky rivulets down her arms. Gaping wounds had been sliced into the crook of her arms; horrible divots that could have fitted a golf ball inside. For a moment I thought I saw worms wriggling out of the holes until I realised they were her veins; Sharon had tugged them through the gashes. I looked down, away from the carnage, only to see I was standing in a pool of blood so deep it was soaking into my shoes. I screamed like I'd never screamed before.

Three officers appeared from nowhere and ordered me out of the cell. 'Code Black!' one barked into her radio as the others tried to wrap Sharon's butchered arms. 'Urgent assistance!'

Three more officers arrived and ordered everyone out of the unit. As I followed the women being herded like sheep, I left footprints of blood across the vinyl floor, a path from Sharon's door out to the front verandah and across the gravel walkway. The women behind me noticed the footprints in front of them, and the women already out there noticed the blood path behind them. All roads led to me. In the muffled background, I heard someone ask what a Code Black was – that day I learned it meant death or serious injury. I was starting to feel a little like Colonel Mustard, with the Carving Knife in the Dining Room. A medical buggy zoomed up the path with nurses and equipment bulging from the sides, and in a matter of minutes Sharon was brought outside on a stretcher, bloodied and bandaged but still alive, and whisked away to the medical centre. Then it was all over.

I hadn't moved. Not a muscle. I was waiting for the officers to follow the bloody footprints to where I stood frozen, and for me to be accused of a crime, while waiting to be tried for another. But the only thing that happened was that I threw up.

I stood there in vomit and blood for another twenty minutes and still no one came for me.

'You over yourself yet, Tucker?' yelled Kristy from the front door. 'We're up for table tennis.'

'Does anyone care about what just happened?' I yelled back, visions of Sharon's mutilated limbs still strobing in my mind.

'What – that you threw up?' she questioned. 'Twice! Get over it and come inside.'

And Kristy was the sensitive one.

I took off my shoes and headed back into A5, where I dumped them in a bucket of soapy water the women had organised to mop up Sharon's lost blood supply.

The suds turned pink and my stomach churned again.

'Hey look, it's Chucka Tucker,' one of the girls teased as I walked in.

'Get fucked,' I replied.

I was already in tears when Shannyn and Sarah ran towards me in the Visitor Centre. From the days they were born I'd never been away from them overnight. Five weeks felt like five years for me, so it must have stretched out like a lifetime for them. Their little bodies crashed into mine as I knelt on the floor, arms outstretched to receive them. Neither girl seemed to care they were in a strange place or that Mummy was dressed in a zip-up green jumpsuit with no pockets – the delightful attire we were required to wear for contact visits. And they could never have known that I'd spent the previous day scrubbing a lady's blood out of my shoes.

'We know you can't come home with us, Mummy. Daddy already told us,' Shannyn said almost sternly, trying to be brave about it. I looked up at my ex-husband and mouthed the words 'Thank you'.

'That's right, my darlings. It might take the judge a little bit of time to decide when I can come home. Mummy is very sorry and very sad that she has had to leave you.' I was raining tears and choking back hard to stop myself from breaking down completely. The girls' father assured them he'd bring them to see me every weekend for as long as it took for the silly old judge to make up his mind. For two hours I cradled my girls like the day they were born. I gently kissed their little faces, wiped away their tears and tucked their soft curls behind their ears. I stroked them with the tips of my fingers, carefully sculpting their features into my memory. Then it was time to go.

'Goodbye, my babies. Mummy loves you more than the stars in the sky and the fish in the sea. It will only be seven more sleeps until we can cuddle again. And Mummy will call you tomorrow. I love you, my little angels . . .'

They started crying and screaming. 'Come with us, Mamma!' They had two officers on either side of them as they were ushered to the door. 'Mummy, you can came home with us now!' Just as they were bundled through the door Shannyn cried out, 'We'll come tomorrow and get you out . . .' And then they were gone.

I will never forget the looks on their faces as they were left to face their strange new world without their mum. I left through the other door and stepped back into my new world to be strip-searched. On the way back to A5 I started packing my emotions away. I was getting good at it and now had a collection of boxes stored right at the back near the base of my skull – one for each emotion: shame, guilt, rage, regret, hate and love. Pure love. Some were neatly tied with ribbons, some were stamped 'Handle with Care' or 'Fragile'. And, of course, there was the big one: 'Open at Own Risk'.

15

TARA

Some stories are so dark and so evil it seemed only fitting to hear them spoken about under the ground. Aired in the daylight or to polite company, they might not be believed. One such story belonged to Tara, a tanned and attractive young girl of twenty-two I'd got chatting to while sharing a cell in the catacombs below Melbourne Magistrates' Court. My case was up for mention and she'd just been arrested over a drug matter. 'Are you out at the prison?' Tara asked through sluggish lips. She was clearly off her face. I smiled and nodded that, yes, I was indeed from the prison.

'I'll be out there soon too,' she murmured.

'Tell me all about yourself, Tara,' I said, settling on the bench next to her. 'How did you get here?'

Tara's father – some kind of Rabbi – started abusing her on the night of her eighth birthday party. She begged her mother to make him stop it but she refused to believe Tara, branding her evil for even saying such a thing. The raping Rabbi didn't stop and at thirteen Tara turned to heroin. She had started menstruating and the possibility of an incestuous pregnancy loomed. Since Tara was of no real use to her father anymore, he banished her from the home to a life on the streets where she sheltered in cardboard boxes in alleys and parking lots. When police inevitably caught up with her, Tara's father smeared her as 'an uncontrollable whore and no daughter of mine'.

The lost little girl found herself a new family – a heavy criminal crew based in Carlton. She lived off the proceeds of petty thefts and nearly every cent went straight up her arm as anaesthetic to a ghastly reality. Even so, people with intent could easily penetrate her feeble narcotic force field and, just before her fourteenth birthday, Tara gave birth to a little girl. The Department of Human Services (DHS) stepped in and removed the baby, Alice, and placed her in the care of Tara's holy and upstanding paedophile father.

'Oh my God,' I said, holding her hand and shaking my head at the tragedy of it. The clatter of a key in the door interrupted us. 'Tucker, you're up,' an officer snapped and ordered me out of the cell where I was handcuffed.

'Ask for me the minute you arrive at the prison,' I urged Tara before I was led to the lift to ascend to the real world.

Paul Galbally smiled at me as I was escorted to the dock. 'How are you going, Kerry?'

By comparison to Tara, I was almost living the dream. 'Oh, I'm OK, Paul. How long will this take?'

'About half an hour,' he replied.

I had decided to plead guilty during my earliest days in the Moorabbin cells and today was about moving that process along. After listening to the police case against me, the judge addressed the room. 'Is there a bail application before the court today?'

'No, your Honour, my client does not seek bail.'

'Will the defendant please stand,' the judge said, motioning for me to rise. 'Kerry Tucker, you have entered a guilty plea and the case will be adjourned to the County Court on a date to be fixed.'

I was glad that part was over – it put me another inch closer to getting back to my girls. I was actually relieved to be herded back into the Brawler for the long drive 'home'. A few days later I was there to welcome Tara on her arrival at Reception. She didn't look as youthful as she had the last time I'd seen her – primarily because she was now hanging out. I set about nursing her through the pain that burned every nerve ending and stripped her of her defences. Soon the worst of her emotional injuries started to show. Tara told me how in the years since giving birth, her contact with Alice had been minimal – her father had seen to that. Now Alice was eight, the same age Tara had been when her father first raped her. At a recent contact visit, Alice told her how 'Grandad is putting his dick in me'. Poor Tara was powerless to act. Nobody believed a junkie – not DHS, not the police and certainly not Tara's mother. To deaden the agony she binged on heroin and pills, bankrolled by a string of violent robberies which is how she came to be back at DPFC.

'Tara,' I said gently, 'you tell me what you want me to do. I'm here for you. I can do whatever you need me to. There is nothing I won't do to help you and your daughter.'

'Thanks, Kerry. I know you care, I can see it in your eyes.'

'Tara, I'm worried about what I don't see in your eyes,' I replied.

That night she quietly slit her throat in her cell and almost bled to death. I know she would have been crushed by her failure to die.

16

LETTERS

My weekly visits with Shannyn and Sarah were my life-blood. It didn't take long, however, for my ex-husband to start complaining over the phone that he didn't have a life anymore and that I should start to consider exactly what I had done to him. Soon, the weekly visits with the girls became fortnightly. The familiar feeling of being trapped and at his mercy came flooding back. Surviving incarceration wasn't a prisoner's only concern; you still needed to manage all the shit that piles into the space you left behind on the outside. A lot of it relates to money.

Paul Galbally had handed his initial $50,000 bill to my family. All of my assets – primarily the house in Healesville – had been frozen and I was uncomfortable that my siblings had been asked to bear the cost. I knew that all of this was my problem and I should solve it myself. In such a bind the average citizen might apply to Legal Aid. After all, they defend anyone. But prisoners know better. Legal Aid runs on a bare minimum of funds, which translates to a bare minimum of legal representation. It was common for women to sit in prison for a year and not meet their lawyer until the day they walked into court. I was also determined not to use Legal Aid because I didn't want to be accused of wasting taxpayers' funds on a defence. In any case, the title of my home was still in my name so technically I was liquid and not entitled to Legal Aid. I needed Paul Galbally.

If I wanted to get out any time soon I had to come up with a plan.

I drafted a five-page letter outlining the legal limbo I was in and then rewrote it twenty times. When I was finally happy I got hold of the Yellow Pages and addressed twenty envelopes to every high-profile Queen's Counsel listed within. I figured if I could secure a prominent QC to act for me pro bono, I would direct them to Paul Galbally in the hope he'd go pro bono too. I got five responses. In the end Philip Dunn QC and my warrior Paul Galbally both agreed to take on my case completely free of charge.

I was striking up more and more friendships with the girls in Remand and had become the A5 'billet' – the inmate responsible for looking after the women and overseeing the food orders.

Food supplied for meals from the prison kitchen to the lock-down units was reasonably good – probably the cheapest meat from Flemington Markets, but prepared by crims in the kitchen it became quite tasty. In 'the cottages' – where the long-term crims lived – women ordered the food and vegies and cooked for themselves.

The fare sold at the DPFC canteen was usually sweet – biscuits, lollies, Coke and soft drink, chocolate, chips, and other sugary rubbish. Thank Christ they also sold toothpaste, shampoo, soap, basic toiletries, cards, stationery and stamps.

Prisoners never handled money. People on your visit list were allowed to deposit up to $120 per month for you to use on phones or at the canteen, which was credited to your account. You would carry your ID number and card all the time and always knew your balance. You also had a weekly allowance – payment for the work you did – which was paid into your account. If you didn't have someone on the outside to drop in extra money each month, you lived off your allowance of $22–36 a week.

The longer we were locked up together, the more protective many of the women became of me. Deeper connections had started to grow. As 30 July rolled around, it brought with it my fortieth birthday. All fifty-two women in A5 threw a surprise party for me. They'd baked two enormous birthday cakes and they all bought a little something from their own funds to put into a birthday box. One girl, Maryanne, had gone to the trouble of having her brother drop $120 into the prison, which she proceeded to spend on me. She stuffed the box full of stamped envelopes, writing pads, toiletries, perfume, lipstick, foundations, mascara, blushers, eye pencils, Milo, cigarettes and one of everything available at the canteen. They organised the barbecue to be brought from the main kitchen and convinced the officers that they should supply the meat. It was as big a night as one can have in a maximum-security prison and I was deeply humbled.

One weekday afternoon I was called to the Visitor Centre where a man was waiting for me. 'Are you Kerry Tucker?' he asked in a reedy, officious voice.

'Yes, I am,' I replied.

'I am here to serve upon your person a Supreme Court writ.'

'Serve upon what?' I queried, scrunching my nose.

'Your person,' he re-stated.

'My *person*?' I echoed, unable to resist mocking him.

'Yes, your person,' he confirmed.

'Would my person be . . . *me*?' I quizzed.

'Yes, it's you, alright? You,' he said getting agitated.

'What is it?' I asked, moving on.

'It's something that you need to treat seriously or you could find yourself in a lot of trouble.'

'Oh, really?' I took a long, careful look around the Visitor Centre and then fixed my eyes back on him. 'Do you think I work here?' I asked flatly. 'I live here. You're standing in a maximum-security prison. Do you think it's possible to get more serious than that?'

'Anything related to the Supreme Court is serious too,' he said and got up to leave. 'Consider yourself served.'

The writ notified me that my home was going to be sold and all proceeds, plus all my other assets, would be confiscated. I hadn't even been sentenced. So there I was, forty years old, with no real way of having a proper relationship with my children, no kind of partner to speak of, no home and nothing to show for myself but a box of goodies from a prison canteen. But, as they always say, life begins at forty.

I can't pinpoint exactly when it happened but sometime during that first year in DPFC I realised I was pretty comfortable being a prisoner. In some ways I felt completely at home. Having never fitted in anywhere else, I somehow clicked in prison. I was useful behind the razor wire; I had responsibilities and a purpose, and people relied on me for help. Not the 'can you grab some milk while you're out?' kind of help – I mean *real* help, of the 'please don't let me die' variety. In spite of the screaming, the bullying, the violence and the human misery all around me I even felt secure in prison. I came to like being locked up. Eventually I came to need it. None of this is to say I was happy.

It was the stuff that happened on the outside that caused me to develop a reputation as being an angry pocket rocket who used her meat cleaver of a tongue to emotionally dice anyone who caused me unnecessary headaches. The situation with the girls' father had become incredibly strained and I'm not proud to say I carried it with me on the compound. Every time I passed a prison phone I'd kick it. I'd had a gutful and I started to become adamant there would be no more caving in – for anyone. If women were being bullied in A5 I took it upon myself to step in and end it, no matter how big or strong the bully was or who her mates were. I had totally shed my sissy-girl, newbie skin.

News about my success in getting a QC to represent me pro bono had caused a stir, and word got around that I possessed an almost magical talent for writing legal letters. 'She's the fucken best – un-fucken-believable,' Tracey testified on my behalf. 'When we were being shat on by the pig dog motherfuckers at Moorabbin cells, Kerry wrote to the Ombudsman! And guess what? The fucken Ombudsman came out and interviewed us. Un-fucken-believable.'

This growing folklore soon resulted in my being approached by every girl in A5 who needed a letter. I had some little successes early on, too; an order granted here, an application accepted by a court there. This only brought more girls in from the compound, and within a month I was preparing letters for nearly half the women ahead of the next visit by the Parole Board. Many of these poor ladies had been robbed of any chance of a formal education and had no idea how to address authority figures. Parole hearings took place three times a year and were a big deal; just like a court hearing complete with judges, magistrates and members of community organisations like Rotary sitting in judgement. Girls would go into the room uneducated, unprepared, ill-informed, grumpy and possibly withdrawing. They felt as if they were on trial all over again, so naturally it didn't take much for them to tell the Parole Board to go and have sex with themselves.

The Board would hear from forty girls per sitting and the success rate was around ten per cent; usually only four or so applicants got released. I was livid when I heard this. I couldn't believe women's sentences were being stretched through nothing more than a lack of organisation and preparation. Some languished behind bars, needlessly, for an extra year!

I took it up with Brendan Money, the General Manager of the prison. He was a genial and warm man in his forties who was always dressed in a suit and tie and clasped his hands neatly in front of him whenever he walked around the prison grounds. He not only knew each inmate's name and details of their history, he knew the names of their children. He radiated goodness, fairness and warmth. I went to him if I needed assistance with anything major or to ensure he was aware of an issue, and he always heard me out.

When I discussed the parole hearings, he agreed there was a problem but explained that he had no internal resources to address it. Fortunately I'd been giving the matter some thought. 'Would it be possible for the women to give written submissions to the board?' I ventured. He didn't see why not.

'OK, tell me your entire life story,' I'd say to the girls during little chats in my cell-cum-office. 'Tell me what happened to you. How did you end up on drugs? How did you wind up committing crimes?' Those interviews would form the basis of our letters (at which I was getting better and better), outlining each individual woman's complicated

114

history and putting a case for why she should be allowed to rejoin society. I'd walk with them to the parole hearing room and wait outside like a nervous parent at a child's tuba recital. 'Remember, be polite and hand them copies of the letter to read,' I'd instruct. 'Do not speak until they ask you questions. In you go. Good luck.' Of course, I never discussed their personal histories with anyone.

Out of the next group of forty applicants, thirty-eight were granted parole and released. As the years rolled on I would sometimes get forty out of forty, but I never dropped under thirty-seven. Almost overnight I became a very important figure in day-to-day prison life. If anyone needed an argument put forward, they were sent to see me. I started doing letters for women's Family Court cases, pleas for leniency, DHS negotiations and Children's Court issues. Sometimes there would be a queue of four or five people milling at my cell door.

Some inmates, however, would prove harder to help than others.

I'd been on an errand in another unit when a brand new first-timer arrived in A5. She was absolutely terrified so the officers asked me to help settle her in. They did not, however, brief me on what had taken place in the thirty minutes I'd been gone. Apparently she had no sooner landed in the unit than she had been physically frisked for smokes and stood over by three different predators. I didn't know this and, when I found her, she was sitting in a corner shaking with fear. I knew just what to do: ask her to go outside so we could have a cigarette and a nice reassuring talk.

'Hello, my name's Kerry and yours is . . . ?' I asked her softly.

No answer. Hmm. Definitely time for that walk in the fresh air and a cigarette.

'Have you got smokes?' I asked, thinking I'd get her some if she didn't.

I never got an answer. In an instant the girl leaped off her chair and ran from the unit with blood-curdling screams. I bolted after her and so did the officers, but she was as fast and nimble as a hare. She bounced here, she darted there, screaming at the top of her lungs the whole time. She spotted a gap in A5's main gate and slipped through it. Now on open ground, she hit top gear and sprinted straight to the outer fence, threw herself onto it and scurried to the top where the razor wire hungrily grabbed hold of her. I could not believe what I was seeing. The girl was now screaming even louder while officers untangled her from the sharp steel rings and took her straight to Medical. The poor thing's arms looked like they'd been put through a food processor.

'What the fuck did you say to her, Tucker?' the officers wanted to know. I explained what I'd said – *and intended by it* – and that's when they told me what had happened earlier on. She must have thought I was going to do the same thing; the proverbial straw that broke the camel's back. Oh, the irony of her being terrified of me – the one inmate in the whole place whose job it was to protect her.

17

BANK MANAGEMENT

I was wandering around the compound one afternoon when I experienced my first Code Aqua. This requires every inmate to return to her cell immediately for a head count and imminent lock-down. In just five minutes, a bustling prison yard teeming with people can be transformed into a ghost town as the women are systematically caged in like battery hens. Code Aqua can be called for any number of reasons, from a fight getting out of control to an escape attempt, a death, serious injury or any whiff of a riot. On this day Code Aqua was triggered by the discovery of speed in the sugar supply. 'Absolutely ingenious,' I thought to myself. Perhaps those responsible hoped it would make our time go faster. Now every grain of amphetamine sugar had to be removed from DPFC. It took all day and we were without regular sugar for the next month.

I was constantly amazed by how the women managed to get drugs into a maximum-security prison. They were downright brilliant. Apart from contraband banked halfway up their vaginas, hypodermic needles would be hidden up there, too; cut down into mini sawn-off syringes that were dismantled and hidden inside the little plastic toy containers you find inside Kinder Surprises. One girl even managed to smuggle in her favourite singlet, her jewellery and enough heroin to do the entire prison for a month. I was learning that often women with massive shipments inside them did so to repay old debts on their return to prison.

The banking system posed a big problem for the prison administration. Fortunately for the inmates, the officers' hands were tied. It would be prohibitively costly to X-ray every single woman upon arrival and, even if they did have the funds for such a system, they'd need a warrant to do it. If officers had a strong and valid reason to suspect a new arrival had swallowed drugs instead, they'd put her in an observation cell in Medical and leave her there. Also known as 'wet cells', these Spartan boxes are under twenty-four-hour surveillance and there's nowhere to hide anything. The blankets are made out of Teflon so there's not even the option of ripping one up to make a noose and stage a 'suicide attempt' in a bid to get out. After about three days, an inmate's body would naturally expel everything. Since there's no avoiding the laws of nature, girls would either have to flush whatever came out down the toilet or they'd be caught with it.

There had once been other less disgusting ways to get drugs in. Apart from hiding them in drinks and nappies, back in the days when the prison was privately run (before the government took over the running of it in 2000), partners and friends of women would apparently just lob heroin- and marijuana-filled tennis balls over the fence. They say the compound could sometimes resemble a warm-up court at the Australian Open.

I could always tell when a shipment of heroin arrived in DPFC. You could walk out onto the compound on a Saturday afternoon and it would be eerily quiet. All the girls would be off their faces and they knew if they dared come out of their unit and stagger about the place the officers would recognise the signs straight away. Punishment for drug use was usually a fine and a stint in 'the slot', another little prison within the prison where girls were locked up for twenty-three hours a day in solitary confinement.

Four days after the opiate wave flooded through the place, all hell would break loose as the girls started to come down and hang out. The screaming would start and the fights would erupt. I got so used to reading these chemical and psychological indicators I could predict changes in the behaviour of the prison population almost down to the hour.

While heroin was the most popular, it was certainly not the only narcotic in DPFC. Women would get high on speed, cocaine and assorted pills. Ecstasy was big in prison during the Noughties, too, as was marijuana. Each group behaved according to their drug of choice. The heroin girls were the easiest to manage when they were stoned; half the time they were 'on the nod', too numb to even hold their heads up. The cocaine kids tended to be higher-class girls; women who worked at the exclusive brothels or the girl-friends of high-flying crims who were importing coke. They tended to just babble like four-year-olds. The women on speed seemed the worst of the bunch. They tended to be aggressive and would pick at their skin and have sores on their faces. Later on, as the ice epidemic took hold, girls would come in so juiced up we weren't allowed in their cells until they'd withdrawn because they could be totally unpredictable and shockingly violent.

In my opinion, however, the worst drug in the place by far was the one they handed out at the Medical Unit. Methadone rots the teeth, leads to excruciating headaches and generally ruins a person's health. Rather than face the horror of a cold-turkey withdrawal from heroin, girls would opt for the government-approved synthetic alter-native to try to wean off it. If a girl had a $2000-a-day heroin habit on the outside, she would begin with, say, a 160ml dose of methadone, which, by the way, is just as addictive as smack. Over the first two weeks that dose would be lowered to 150ml, then to 140ml for a month or so, 130ml for six months, and so on. Even those tiny adjustments would trigger a wave of terrible withdrawal symptoms. As a result it wasn't uncommon for a prisoner who started on a 160ml dose to take five years to be weaned off altogether.

At any given time at least eighty per cent of inmates in DPFC were on some kind of medication, dispensed daily in Medical. Some were prescribed valium for anxiety, some needed antidepressants, some were on the methadone program, others were prescribed Largactil – a powerful and stupefying anti-psychotic drug that put women into a kind of waking coma. I could always tell when someone was on it because she'd develop 'the Largy shuffle' – a pathetic, bombed-out gait which was about as fast as your average garden snail.

Alarmingly, women would take anything they could get their hands on, happily trading their stash for whatever pills the next girl might have scored from Medical. Chemical cocktails were tipped down throats with gay abandon, causing who knows what damage. The sister of a famous AFL player came into A5 one day and proved to be seriously deranged. 'Drug fucked', they called it. She was only twenty or twenty-one at the time but was so scrambled by poly-drug use that she spent her days walking in circles deep in conversation with herself. She'd often plonk down next to me for hours on end, sensing that I cared about her and would protect her. Being in such close prox-imity to wrecked people like her reminded me how grateful I was that I'd never fallen into the bottomless sink-hole of drug abuse.

While it was all well and good to be stoned on the Vic-torian Government's supply, there were harsh consequences for anyone caught using contraband. The officers, better known as the 'Piss Police', conducted urine tests, and anyone who failed was hauled to Governor's Court where one of the prison governors questioned them about where they got it. (This was really just a formality because most of the time the code of silence kicked in.) Offenders were then escorted to the slot for solitary confinement.

Still, the women had ways of staying one step ahead. One day I was struck by the strange contents in the food supply crates outside the unit. The first one contained carrots, cabbages, some crappy cuts of meat and *sixty-five lemons*! 'Who ordered sixty-five lemons?' I asked. It was explained to me that pure lemon juice flushes traces of drugs out of the system. 'It might be hard to force it down the hatch,' one girl told me, 'but your next urine test will come back squeaky clean.' It seemed to take a while before the officers cottoned on – they must have thought we had some killer recipes using lemons.

One girl came into DPFC charged with importing a gutful of cocaine. She'd arrived on a flight from South Africa and the Federal Police had nabbed her at Melbourne Airport. She was X-rayed and rushed into surgery because the packages she'd swallowed were degrading and she was in danger of dying by the mother of all overdoses. Doctors cut her wide open, retrieved the narcotics and sewed her back up so she could face the music. Once she had recovered sufficiently she was shipped out to Deer Park where it was my job to receive her.

'Hello,' I said smiling. 'I'm Kerry. How are you feeling? Have you got a good lawyer?'

'Why? I don't need one,' she replied.

'Possum,' I said evenly, 'you've been caught red-handed bringing several kilos of cocaine into Australia. It's a fairly serious thing here. You might want to think about getting a lawyer.' I was being completely level with her, trying to prepare her to face the reality that she was unlikely to get out any time soon without good legal counsel. But she just looked back at me with a slight air of disbelief.

'What do you mean? It's my word against theirs!'

I couldn't believe her naivety. 'Didn't they slit you open from your throat to your vagina?' I asked. 'I'm guessing their word is pretty good.'

'Yeah, still, it's their word against mine. I'll plead not guilty and see how I go.'

I shook my head. 'Really? Look, you might want to get a lawyer because the police are –'

'Nup!' she cut in. 'They've got nothing.'

'It sounds like they've got quite a bit of evidence . . .'

'Only the cocaine.'

'That'll usually do it – but give it your best shot anyway,' I said before walking away.

Needless to say she was with us for a while.

On the opposite end of the drug-smuggling spectrum was a darling lady from South Australia. She was sixty-five and had been on her own since her husband died years earlier. As sometimes happens, she went online and met a nice, upstanding Nigerian fellow and the poor thing agreed to fly over to South Africa to meet him. He told her he loved her, that she was the woman of his dreams and how they would always be together. He promised that after she returned to Australia they'd make arrangements to get married.

Of course they would!

When she got off the plane in Melbourne she, too, was caught with a huge amount of narcotics carefully hidden in her luggage. Unlike Miss Cocaine Guts, the South Australian lady was the very definition of an unwitting drug mule. It was heartbreakingly sad to see this lonely, vulnerable and innocent woman locked up with actual criminals. Anyone and everyone could see she'd had no idea about the drugs – everyone except the Australian Federal Police.

I was so angry that her life was ruined by a scammer looking to make some easy money but too gutless to risk his own hide in prison. I pushed hard to contact her family and get a defence moving. Every day she'd come to see me and say, 'Thank you, dear,' but part of her held on to the fantasy that had been sold to her. I just wanted somebody to *do* something to catch the real perpetrator. Finally, frustrated that I could do nothing more, I sat down with her. 'Listen,' I said, 'why don't you let me give the prison your Nigerian friend's name so we can put him on the visitor list? That way if he wants to come to see you the prison will have cleared it.'

'Oh, he'd be horrified if he knew I was in prison,' she replied.

'Well, at least you'd have the chance to see him again,' I said, trying to sound optimistic about the faux romance.

With that she gave me the bastard's name and I promptly wrote to her family and shared it with them. Thankfully she was eventually released and the charges dropped – but not before she'd lost several months of her life to a prison cell. I hope it spelled the end of her internet romances.

18

CHANGING CODE

Outside of drugs, food was the No. 1 priority for most women in DPFC, and as the A5 billet it was my problem when women started complaining that they weren't getting their daily serves of yoghurt. It didn't take long to work out a crim named Michelle was the blockage in the dairy supply line. She had taken it upon herself to ration A5's yoghurt, but instead of giving it to their rightful (and hungry) owners, she was handing it out to her mates in other units on the compound. Michelle lived on B Side of Remand, and although I was a lowly A-Side dweller she liked me and we got along quite well. Still, my heart was in my mouth as I approached her in the common area.

'Hello, Michelle!' I said. 'Hey, the girls are saying they're not getting their yoghurt and I can see that food is a pretty big thing around here so . . . what in the fuck is going on?'

'None of your business,' she snorted from the couch.

'Well, it is my business because I live here now and I'm going to be here for a while – a bit longer than you.'

I might as well have poked a snake. Michelle was on her feet in a flash. Outraged that I had dared question her sentence, she stormed out onto the compound growling threats through gritted teeth.

The length of a woman's sentence is a major factor in how much standing she has in the prison. The women doing twenty years for murder cast an enormous shadow over those who are in for relatively minor crimes – and on much shorter sentences. Michelle had told everyone she was serving four years for a violent assault; quite a significant stretch that afforded her a certain cachet among the other crims. But I had it on good authority from an officer that she was, in fact, due to be released in six months. What's more, hers was what's known as a 'bullshit crime' – some kind of minor fracas.

A few minutes later Michelle was back in the unit trailing a group of her tough, yoghurt-fed mates from the compound. Suddenly I was extremely worried about Michelle's propensity for violence, no matter how 'bullshit' it might have been. 'She's talking shit about my sentence and trying to undermine my fucking rights and disrespecting me,' she said, jabbing a finger at me.

'No, I'm just trying to stop you from fucking everyone over,' I replied as calmly as I could. I was terrified, but, as ever, I felt I had already lost everything that was dear to me. Michelle and her cronies couldn't make my life any worse than it already was. I was damned if I was going to let her bully the food right out of people's mouths, so I let rip with mine. I stepped up close and whispered in her ear, 'You're not doing four years. You and I both know you'll be able to buy all the yoghurt you want when you get out in six months. But right now, everyone else in here – who isn't going home – needs their fucking food, OK?'

There was a long silence as Michelle assessed her options. Finally she stepped back and defaulted to the threat of violence. 'Do you wanna take it outside, Tucker?' she asked, oozing menace. It was the first time I felt genuinely afraid of being bashed by another woman.

'No thanks, I'd rather stand here and talk to you about when it is that you're going home.'

'Four years!' she bellowed.

'Are you sure about that?' By then about twenty-five women had gathered to watch the stand-off. 'Do you want to consider that again, Michelle, because what it's going to do is show everyone here that you're a liar and a coward.' Michelle's mates started to lose interest and peel away. Soon Michelle's tough-girl veneer did too. Now with no one to back her up she confessed that some of the old-timers on the compound had forced her to get the yoghurt for them.

'So you were being bullied?' I asked.

'Yeah.'

'Feels shit, doesn't it?'

She didn't answer.

'OK, why don't we just all get our yoghurt and forget this ever happened,' I said. Unsurprisingly the old-timers found out Michelle had given them up about the yoghurt racket and bullied her some more. At least she only had to cop it for another six months. The episode was a dismal reminder of the culture of stand-over. Everywhere I looked I saw bullying. Not only did I detest it, I struggled to understand it. Virtually every single one of these women had been victims of violence, bullying and abuse at the hands of some male cretin or other. For them to then turn around and start doing the same thing to another woman – whose suffering was no different from theirs – was just plain stupid and I told them so. Once, I became so outraged I even broke the almighty code: 'Speak no evil' . . .

Feuds were commonplace among inmates, and although violence would occasionally break out, psychological attacks could take an even greater toll – as Miss Crime Family had found out in the Moorabbin drunk tank. Sometimes, however, women chose to settle scores in the most heinous and disgusting ways imaginable. One day I was told that a girl had tried to get back at someone by wiping her menstrual blood on the rival's muffin. I almost retched at the thought of it and marched into A5 to explain to the entire unit what had happened. I then went to the unit supervisor and told him that all the girls were aware. I knew it was just a matter of time before they acted under 'duty of care'. I also told Bloody Mary what to expect for her revolting act.

'How do we know this filthy little creature hasn't got HIV?' I complained to the supervisor. During lunch muster, A5 was locked down and Bloody Mary was escorted to Protection. So there – evil spoken. It was the only time I ever set someone up to an officer – *the* No. 1 big no-no of the prison code. But I paid no price for it whatsoever. The way I saw it, if your code was about protecting women who would do such a thing to another inmate then it was a fairly crap arrangement. No one really argued the point.

It was one thing to confront bullying head on, but to truly deal with it I felt I had to try to change the culture. Over the course of a few weeks I mapped out a draft for my own DPFC Orientation Program to be run in the A5 Remand/Reception Unit. I put a submission to Brendan Money and prison management, outlining the pros and cons of the program versus the status quo of the existing prisoner code. One potential obstacle was the fact I didn't want officers present during the sessions because it would defeat the purpose of allowing the women to speak freely. I could have used such an opportunity to convince women to riot or train them to spit at the officers, but management knew I wouldn't. They trusted me and I was given the go-ahead.

At regular Sunday night sessions I'd address all the new arrivals about what it was like to live in DPFC and what the accepted practices among the inmates were. I usually began by advising them not to give the officers any grief. 'The smart way is to get officers onside and treat them with respect,' I'd say. 'Then you can expect to be cut some slack with most things. Do your time in prison smart. It's not smart to do your sentence in the slot.'

I'd go to great lengths to drill it into them that bullying and intimidation of any kind would not be tolerated by the inmates or the officers. 'The officers may slot you, but the women will deal with you on another level,' I warned. I educated them to respect each other's differences and each other's traumas. 'Do your own sentence. Don't judge the women in Protection, because you know nothing about them or their personal stories. It's not acceptable to call them dogs.' I challenged every bit of 'old school' culture, but did it in a respectful, constructive way. And by educating new arrivals they, in turn, carried the new culture out onto the compound. Slowly but surely it started to have an effect. Tempers still flared and women still tried to put it over others but, by and large, the prevailing attitude became more respectful and women felt a little safer inside the prison. The tragedy was there was nothing I could do to help the women once they left.

Debbie Singh was a lovely woman who hailed from Swan Hill near my old hometown of Robinvale. Debbie was in on drugs charges and for six months I listened to her harrowing tales of life with a violent and abusive partner. She was dreading going back to him, but she was an addict and had no one else to 'look after' her so she gravitated to him like a moon to a black hole. When the day came for her to leave DPFC I walked with her to the gates and waved her goodbye. 'Seeya, Deb. You're gonna be OK. You'll be fine. Take care of yourself and write to me. B-y-y-y-e-e-e!'

Nine days later she was dead. The Salvation Army came to see me and told me Debbie had left a note saying, 'Tell Kerry that it wasn't going to happen for me.' Deb had overdosed and her death was treated as a suicide, but her body had also been covered in bruises. I was in shock. The wonderful, broken, sweet and fragile girl I'd come to love in just seven months behind bars together, was suddenly lost to the world forever. I ran around the compound grabbing hold of people and shaking them: 'Oh my God, Debbie's dead! She's dead! Do you hear me?' But everyone seemed to be used to it, whereas Debbie was the first friend I lost. After a while Deb became Shari, who became Betty, who became Jenny, who turned into a long roll call of dead women.

Deep down, though, I knew Deb had stood a fair chance of taking her own life on the outside. We had talked a lot about her problems. In less than a year I had become something of a seer among the inmates at DPFC; a kind of 'woman whisperer' who could predict behaviour and actions long before events caught up with my hunches. I could tell who would get into trouble within the first few days or weeks of their arrival, and I could tell who wouldn't. I'd watch women from the moment they walked into Reception and make careful mental notes about their body language and their spoken words – right down to their tone, pitch and flow. I'd listen to what they told me first and what they chose to tell me last. I knew if they had serious issues, health problems, mood imbalances, depression or PTSD (post-traumatic stress disorder).

I'd sit with women and stare into their eyes to see if they connected with mine. I always tried to convey a sense of safety with my gaze; to let her know I was genuine and open and that I took her care seriously. I could sense a lot by looking women in the eyes. They were indeed windows to their souls and I could tell whether her soul was 'good' or 'bad' or whether it was just vacant for the moment. At all times I focused on being unthreatening. My voice was always warm, soft and smooth and I made my hand gestures as graceful as I could. I was slow, deliberate, reassuring, comforting, quiet and steady. Whenever I touched them I was gentle but not lingering; reassuring but not overly familiar. I read and respected women's individual body language and found it often spoke louder than any words.

If a woman told me she wanted to kill herself, I had enough knowledge, history and insight to know if she meant business or was merely seeking attention. It was crucial because what I did next would have a direct impact on her life at that moment. If I knew it was a genuine threat she would end up 'wet-celled' with a Teflon blanket. In that case, I'd make sure it was me who explained what was about to happen to her and not an officer. She would trust me if I said they weren't going to hurt her but I'd still point out that the experience wasn't going to be nice.

If a woman made an empty suicide threat and she was wet-celled regardless, then the experience would be soul destroying and she'd never trust me again. It was therefore better that I help her work through whatever problem she was having rather than involve the officers. These were life and death decisions, but I felt comfortable making them because I knew every single woman, their personalities and their past behaviours. It became obvious why they wanted to keep me in Remand.

19

HIERARCHY

The prison was like a giant filing cabinet for malfunctioning humans. Everyone was labelled and sorted into their specific genus or subgroup. Inmates were assigned status according to an age-old social algorithm that took account of everything, from the nature of their crime and the length of their sentence to their criminal pedigree, their personality, propensity for violence, their trustworthiness, sense of humour and their personal failings.

The units were organised into seven main sections. A5 was like a massive sorting drawer where new arrivals were kept in single lock-down cells while they settled in and were sorted. After that they were moved out of A5 and generally into the B Units, which contained twelve open cells. A6 was the Psychiatric Unit; A7 was Protection; A1 was a single-cell lock-down unit where women were released from the slot. And then there was the slot itself.

The C Units were the most comfortable in the prison – reserved for women who would be in DPFC for a long time. Also known as 'the cottages', C Units were individual buildings, about the size of a holiday shack, where five women lived communally together and were even allowed to cook their own food.

In prison, everything and everyone was clearly labelled with either numbers, letters, colours or shapes and assigned a place in the hierarchy – the officers were no exception. Like any other tiered organisation, the prison was managed from the top down. As general manager, Brendan Money sat atop the structure. He delegated the day-to-day running of the prison to a group of three to four prison 'governors'. The governors wore impressive shiny uniforms with a crown on their shoulder to really signify who was in charge. I dealt a lot with Governor Wayne Blyth and Governor Tracy Jones (now the general manager) and I have a great deal of respect for them and warm memories. We went to them when the three-pippers blocked us or the two-pippers appeared to have slipped into a coma. They were no fools and were fair in their dealings. I also enjoyed their humour.

The governors, in turn, managed the officers who managed us. These Corrections Officers – the people we had to interact with most on a day-to-day basis – were also categorised according to rank. The most junior officers were identified by a single dot, or 'pip', on their shoulders while the more experienced officers had two dots and the veteran Corrections Officers boasted three. In much the same way that prisoners of different status behaved according to their 'rank', the officers also varied depending on how many pips were sewn onto their shirts. The junior officers tended to try to make friends with the prisoners but whenever an inmate was pulled into line by a 'one-pipper', they normally treated the officer with a measure of contempt. 'You're just a newbie, so why don't you fuck off?' they'd snarl. Given that new officers were minted after just six weeks' training, it was understandable that inmates felt they needed to earn some respect before they started dishing out orders. When they became two-pippers, however, the tables turned. Suddenly they didn't want to be our buddies anymore. In prison, two can play at that game and our attitude was, 'We're not going to help you along the way so you can fuck off too.'

If they survived long enough, an officer would become a three-pipper and their evolution from ape into an actual human being would be complete. The senior officers were generally a pleasure to deal with; people like Miss Johnson who were calm, fair, intelligent and professional. Even so, I rarely trusted the officers with serious or sensitive information. I would always either go to the governors (mainly Tracy Jones or Wayne Blyth), Mr Bennett (the head of prison security known as the Collator), or the wise and unflappable Brendan Money. All knew how to protect information – particularly when a leak could jeopardise someone's safety. Once I worked out where everyone sat in the pecking order – both the crims and our keepers – it was relatively easy to negotiate the prison system. Soon I was on the move.

The Remand Unit is the most volatile place in DPFC, by far. A good thing it's fenced off from the rest of the prison. Fortunately the average inmate was transferred out of there and into one of the other units after seven or eight weeks. I ended up staying for eighteen months. Not only did I *want* to remain in A5, management was happy to keep me in there because it was obvious I was having a positive impact. Throughout that time I became firm friends with Andrea Mohr, the lovely German peer support worker who'd comforted me on my first day. Because of her job, Andrea could access A5 at will and we spent a fair bit of time together. She was funny, highly intelligent and – as a former international drug courier – quite well travelled and exotic. I truly adored her and always will, but all too soon (for me, anyway) they had to let her go.

As a long-term inmate, Andrea had spent the last leg of her sentence in the C Units – one of the six self-contained 'cottages' at the south end of the compound. Since they were reserved mostly for women serving long sentences, the cottages housed plenty of murderers. Actually 'cottage' is probably too cute a word to describe them; they're fairly Spartan boxes built out of concrete besser bricks and topped with an iron roof. There was a kitchen and a common area with a TV, and a hallway with five small cells running off it.

While the women had a certain amount of autonomy, there were still surveillance cameras mounted everywhere and the prisoners were locked in their cells at 7pm in summer and 5pm in winter, like everybody else. Even so, cottages were considered the top of the tree when it came to a small measure of privacy and respect among other inmates.

Andrea tried to get me to move into the C Units whenever a place became available, but I always demurred, preferring to stay in my trusty old cell in A5. When a bed came up in her cottage in C2B she really put the pressure on. It was up to the other inmates in her unit to pick and choose who they accepted. The reason was obvious: women living under pressure in such close proximity needed to get along reasonably well. Just as in polite society, you wouldn't choose to rent a flat with someone you dearly wanted to punch in the face. It was most unusual for women to move from Remand, bypass the other A and B Units (where the bulk of the inmates lived) and go straight to the cottages. But I had more than paid my dues in Remand and was one such lucky girl.

Andrea had taken me under her wing and vouched for me among the long-termers. She was also aware of the work I was doing to help the women in A5. 'You really should do the peer support training and make it official,' Andrea said one day. I completed the next twelve-week course in prison peer support, but the fact was I had already done much of it on my own initiative in A5. In reality, no matter what training you had, the only way you could be a peer support worker in DPFC was if you had the respect and trust of the other inmates. Now – after nineteen months of holding their trembling hands, mopping their brows, writing their letters and standing up for their rights – I did.

I felt more supported and valued in prison than I ever did in free society, and although my move to the cottages was assured, the women in A5 begged me to stay. It was strange to think that to most Australians I was a faceless low-life criminal – someone to be shunned – but in my tiny world behind the razor wire I was not only important, I was doing some real good. I was helping to improve people's lives. Even some of the officers would confide in me, and I repaid them – as I did the inmates – by never breaking a confidence. Compassion and a sense of humour are good character traits to have, but trust is the most valued commodity in prison.

As a freshly minted peer educator my role became formalised. Each day I would be paged to Reception where any number of girls might have arrived overnight or during the day. I would meet with them and explain what would happen as they entered the system at DPFC. I was allowed to sit with them in their cells, even in the Medical Unit which was a strict no-go zone for other prisoners because of access to drugs. Most of all, I would reassure them that they were going to be safe. After that, anything could happen in a day in the life of a peer support worker. I'd be called on if someone had overdosed, if they were refusing to leave their cell, if there had been a fight, if someone had self-harmed, if they were going berserk, if someone was having a breakdown, if a prisoner in the slot had requested

Here I am at two years of age in 1965. I always struggled to belong and in many ways became used to being alone.

This is one of the only photographs I have of my whole family. We're at my eldest sister Lynette's wedding in 1973. *From back left:* Cheryl, older brother Terry, Mum, Garry (my brother-in-law), Lynette, Dad and Kathy. I'm the flower girl in the front and my younger brother, Tony, is the pageboy.

My class photograph, 1975. I'm in the back row, third from right. Later, at high school, I was elevated by two full academic years so that I was no longer with my peers.

At the ripe old age of sixteen in Robinvale, Victoria.

For my twenty-fifth birthday I was given a surprise party, in Healesville. As you can see, I totally embraced the *Dynasty* look!

My wedding day in 1990 was a complete disaster – mostly thanks to me. I was the Bridezilla from hell.

Sarah, around three years old, in 2000. From the earliest age she was strong and resilient.

I was a clucky mum who fussed over Sarah and Shannyn's every need and loved every second of it. This photograph was taken in 2002 – just before I was jailed for much of their childhood.

Shannyn, my glorious dark-haired little girl, at around eight months in 1995. She grew up to be the spitting image of me, complete with wise-cracking attitude and fiery temperament.

Even in prison I was never the shy and retiring type. In this photograph, which was taken by a female officer, I'm in the so-called 'leisure centre'.

In my cell looking at photographs of Sarah and Shannyn, who I missed terribly. *Photograph courtesy of John Krutop*

I was allowed two twelve-minute phone calls per week to my children (six minutes per daughter). Here, I'm on the phone directly opposite my unit – C2B. *Photograph courtesy of John Krutop*

With the encouragement of my friend and tutor Carolyn Beasley, I set about writing a book called *Rhiannon & Sasha Visit Mum* to educate the children of female inmates. It's still used in prisons and legal firms in Victoria today.

The wise and unflappable prison general manager Brendan Money. He was a genial and warm man who knew each inmate's name and the details of their history, along with the names of their children. *Photograph courtesy of* Australian Story

When I completed my Master of Arts, the full university graduation ceremony was the first to be held inside an Australian prison. To the far left of me is Professor Kay Lipson, the then dean of Lilydale Campus, who made my PhD and then job at Swinburne University possible. Next to her is the then Swinburne vice chancellor, Dale Murphy.

After a tearful farewell at the gate, my sister Cheryl collected me on 9 November 2007 and I was driven away from Deer Park for the last time. I felt as if I was in a dream.

Saying goodbye to some of the officers.

My first lunch of freedom in a fabulous waterfront restaurant with my sister Cheryl. Members of my family were there and I was fussed over, though it took a while to adjust. The wine helped!

Cheryl *(left)*, Joylene *(centre)* and Sharon *(behind the camera)* booked us into a rooftop apartment in Docklands for my first night.

I came to value, trust and totally adore Carolyn Beasley – the Swinburne University tutor (now acting head of department) who came to the prison to teach us every Friday.

Hosting Melbourne Inspiration Day, 2017, in which I decided to really open up about how much Sarah and Shannyn have inspired me.

Reunited with my precious girls. *Photograph by Alana Landsberry, courtesy of Bauer Media Limited*

Today Sarah *(left)* is a very talented singer and Shannyn *(below)* is a wonderful hairdresser and colourist.

I made a promise to make my daughters proud of me again one day, but in truth it's they who have made me proud.

me or if an inmate in Protection was having problems and needed support. And, inevitably, there were all those girls in withdrawal to look after, and endless parole and legal letters to write.

Some days I would receive girls who had been transferred from the Youth Training Centre (YTC) – and I mean 'girls'. On those days it was hard not to feel frustrated and angry because the world was so cruel. While in reality they were at least eighteen years old, some inmates from YTC could have passed for thirteen. Some were Wards of the State and some hadn't even been convicted of crimes, but all of them were studies in neglect and sadness. They always proved to be a handful, too. At YTC they had been at the top of the tree but now they were in the Big Girls' School, so they'd try to run riot in a silly, youthful attempt to convince everyone they were tough and cool. 'Drop the attitude,' I would snarl at them. 'We'll look after you in here but you have to cut the bullshit and behave as you're told.'

It always took me two to three times as long to settle the YTC girls in. These poor kids had just about grown up by the time they were fourteen, and often had kids of their own by fifteen. I sure knew that was an easy mistake to make. When they arrived in prison at eighteen they were pretty much old-school crims. Many of them had lived hard on the streets from the time they were ten or younger, and life had turned them into vicious little girls – on the outside at least. As soon as I'd sit down, take their hand and say, 'How can I help you?' they'd dissolve into tears.

Some of them were so small their feet would swing in the air as they sat on the edge of their bed. Others were clearly still developing and I wouldn't have been surprised if they believed in the Tooth Fairy. 'It's going to be OK,' I'd tell them. 'I won't let anyone else hurt you. You'll be safe in here.' But I knew that promise only extended as far as the front gate. Once they were released they'd be on their own. Some would come back to prison. Some I'd never see again. Others would die out there.

Whenever I met a new arrival the first thing I would do would be to suss them out for any injuries. 'Hi, I'm Kerry,' I'd begin and give them a warm smile. 'I'm a prisoner here. I'm one of you. How are you feeling? Are you hurt at all?' I'd assess her physically as I went. I might touch her arm or hold her hand. 'I'm here for you,' I'd continue, 'and I don't care what you've done. You don't have to tell me a thing, but whatever you say in here stays with me, OK?'

I'd scan for track marks or other tell-tale signs of drug addiction or indicators of a mental disturbance. Some women remained pretty quiet in the cells while others saw me as a sounding board and suddenly felt compelled to unburden themselves. On those occasions Reception was just like confession at St Joseph's in Leeton, only I was cast in the role of Father and the women's sins were very, very real. I was given first-hand accounts of crimes ranging from shoplifting to multiple murder. Some women went into the goriest of details. Some even told me where they'd dumped their victims' bodies. A few nights after one such chat I was relaxing in front of the 6pm news, watching police fish a corpse out of a pond on the city outskirts, when I sat bolt upright. 'Oh my God! That must be Neale!' I figured I was possibly the only person in Victoria who knew that if Neale hadn't been such a frightening, wife-beating monster he might not be so dead.

Naturally there were a lot of women I welcomed at DPFC who I couldn't stand. That's not a judgement – just a statement of fact, and I'm quite sure I wasn't everybody's cup of tea either. But there were more than a few who I really liked. Despite their miserable life stories and the shit cards they had been dealt, some women were just really pleasant human beings. They were fun and smart and, somehow, they remained optimistic. One woman I got to know had first been raped when she was six but she *still* had ambitions for a better life. Like a lot of women in prison, a white picket fence featured prominently in her dreams. To me the fact she was still breathing was miracle enough. She was typical of the women I was most drawn to – the lowly ones who were never given the first chance; the women who could have been forgiven had they given up long ago. I was fiercely protective of them and I wanted to be there for them, always. That was wishful thinking, and God only knows what eventually happened to that woman. I don't know how long someone like that can keep her chin up. I truly hope she's happy and safe somewhere behind a white picket fence, but I doubt it.

At the other end of the spectrum were women who would never find peace, or even know what it was; the ones who would likely never fit back into society. When I first met Sarah Cheney she appeared totally sane to me, despite the fact she was in prison for viciously attacking a random woman with a knife at La Trobe University. Sarah was being kept in Isolation and I spent time in there talking with her about her parents, her life and how she was trying to work out where she was in the world. Within two days she appeared to go completely insane. Sarah managed to get her hands on some paperclips and tried to use them to gouge her eyeballs out. It was just the beginning of violence towards herself and others in DPFC. In hindsight I was lucky I got her on a good day. According to one recent press report she's now considered 'Australia's most dangerous inmate' and she's still in Isolation today.

20

JANICE

Some inmates had no business whatsoever being locked in a prison.

Janice appeared to have Down's syndrome and had the intelligence of a ten-year-old. The problem was she kept committing adult crimes and, since she was actually thirty-five, the courts kept sending her back to prison. We first got acquainted in the cells beneath the city where we'd both faced court earlier in the day. As sometimes happened, the Brawlers were stretched to capacity so we got stranded underground past lock-down at 7pm. That's when I was told we weren't going to make it back home until much later and were instead going to spend some time at the Melbourne Custody Centre. The very name sent a chill up my spine.

The Custody Centre was a notorious and terrifying place. As the main reception point for people arrested in the city, it's a world unto itself and considered something of a wild frontier compared to the relative order at DPFC. The officers there must have been hand-picked from those who scored the lowest in the psych test and highest in brutality. They were cruel, all of them, and they were allowed to be. Nobody else really knew what happened in the Custody Centre or even cared. At the various court holding cells around Melbourne there was usually someone present from the Salvation Army or the Red Cross but not at the Custody Centre – no one was allowed in there except for mean-spirited police and Corrections Officers, and prisoners they could bash with impunity.

I couldn't show Janice how scared I was; she was already crying about having to 'go for a ride in a dark van'. I was fiercely protective of her and I feared she would attract the attention of the psychopath officers at the Custody Centre. As we were marched inside I clutched her hand as if I was walking her to pre-school. It was like stepping onto another planet: the air was different, the light was different and the walls seemed to moan. The officers slumped against the main counter as if they were hanging at the sleaziest bar in Australia. They leered at us and one even adjusted his tackle right in front of Janice. We were ushered into a large damp holding cell that had a blackboard on the door chalked with the words 'Babysitting two women'. Once inside we were assailed by the reek of an open toilet that was overflowing with sanitary pads and faeces. Over the next couple of hours we had to listen as the officers belted the crap out of a guy in the cell next door. This only made Janice cry even louder.

'Janice!' I hiss-whispered. 'Janice, you need to shut up! They'll come for us if you don't be quiet!'

This only made matters worse. Janice regressed into being a blubbering baby. When she got really nervous or upset she would suck her mouth in and out and make a little popping noise like a cartoon fish: '*Mwop-mwop-mwop-mwop . . .*'

'What the fuck is going on with those fucking things from the County Court?' an angry voice boomed down the hallway.

'*Janice! Shut up!*' I pleaded as urgently and quietly as I could.

But the poor thing kept right on with her fish impression. Terrified that we were going to invoke the ire of the slap-happy policemen, I clamped my hand over Janice's mouth. '*Shhh!*' She started biting my fingers so I pressed against her mouth even harder. And each time she'd stick her tongue out through my fingers. I couldn't believe it; what had started out as a daytrip into court had ended in a stinking inner-city gulag where I was in danger of smothering a fellow inmate to death or being bashed by Victoria's lowest law-enforcement officers. Finally, they beat our male neighbour into silence, which only brought Janice's sucking sounds into sharp relief.

'Don't you fucking make me come down there and open that door,' the voice thundered again. 'Trust me, that's the last thing you want.'

I could not have agreed more. As if by miracle, a Brawler arrived soon after to drive us back out to DPFC in the late evening. We had spent just over two hours in the Custody Centre. It had felt like a year.

At Deer Park the disturbed and particularly needy inmates tended to flock to me like moths to a flame. Janice went a step further. The following day, she pretty much adopted me as her mother. Wherever I went, she wanted to go. Whenever I lit a cigarette, she immediately sparked one up, too. Whatever make-up I put on, she would put on. It quickly became the prison joke. I warned people not to tease her or touch her under any circumstances. 'She's not really an adult,' I said. 'She shouldn't be in here.' I couldn't understand why she was in prison in the first place.

'Janice,' I asked her as we sat and lit another smoke at precisely the same time, 'what are you doing in here? What was your crime?'

'I needed a smoke,' she began, holding hers up as if to underscore she meant a cigarette. 'I went in to this store and I saw they left the cash drawer open. I jumped the counter, got the money and took off. I got caught really quickly, though. Someone must have given me up.'

'Riiight, so what kind of store was it?' I pressed.

'Don't really know, but when I walked in there were cameras everywhere, lights bleeping and that. I think it was a camera shop.'

It had, in fact, been a security and surveillance equipment retailer. No fewer than forty-three operational cameras captured Janice's brazen heist, which she had been oblivious to. 'I honestly don't know how they got me,' she said with a puzzled shake of her head. 'But they came around and arrested me real quick.'

'Janice,' I said as we stubbed out our smokes in choreographed unison, 'it's going to remain one of life's great mysteries.'

It goes without saying Janice hadn't been born with a penchant for crime. Her parents had given up on her and she was sent away. As a vulnerable teenager, she was easily manipulated and ended up being raped by a man who deployed her to commit thefts and burglaries to finance his drug habit. And now she was in jail paying the price for his wanton evil acts.

The more I stuck up for Janice, the more I became a god to her, and whenever she fucked up, I was the person the inmates would complain to. I remained her ferocious defender – even when she urinated in the prison pool. Of course, nobody would have known about it had Janice not told everyone. The other prisoners were furious and even the long-termers were losing patience. 'Kerry, you have to do something,' they warned. So I took Janice aside and sat her down like a mum with a little girl who didn't know better.

'Janice, you can't wee in the pool – ever. OK? What's going to happen now, sweetheart, is I'm forbidding you from going into that pool for two weeks.'

'OK. I'm sorry, Kerry.'

The pool wasn't really much of a concern at DPFC. For a start, no one had any bathers so if you went in it'd be in shorts and a shirt. It was often off limits because the officers didn't want to bother supervising us and most of the time inmates were too busy anyway. If you weren't working you were being mustered or lining up for medication or having visiting time. Weekends tended to be the only time there was an opportunity to really use it, but weekends were usually when the drugs were in so girls didn't go swimming for fear of drowning. Besides, nobody liked to think they were paddling around in urine.

Two weeks later, Janice came running up to me with a towel over her shoulder. 'Kerry, it's been two weeks. Can I go back into the pool?' she asked.

I had forgotten all about it. 'Oh my God, of course you can. But remember, you cannot wee in the pool. And if you do, don't tell everyone. Got it?'

'Got it, Kerry.'

Janice kept coming back to prison, time after time. I'd get wind of it before her arrival, because the officers knew it would be a good idea if I was mentally prepared for the extra responsibility. Her second visit to Deer Park was punishment for a stunt she pulled at Frankston train station. Janice was bored and lonely and thought she could solve this by using her mobile phone to ring 000 and say there was a riot in full swing and people were being killed on the platform. The police sent ten patrol cars and a helicopter to the scene. Janice thought it was just terrific . . . until they traced the hoax call to her phone.

At least when she was in prison she had me, which pretty much guaranteed no harm would come to her. The authorities said they had no other options; they couldn't just let her loose on Melbourne to commit robberies and cause chaos. Somebody could get hurt, including poor Janice. They couldn't rightly put a thirty-five-year-old in YTC, either, because the mean, street-smart little girls in there would eat her alive. Even so, after her second arrest I went to Brendan Money. 'I know it's complicated but she shouldn't be in here,' I said. 'She's a ten-year-old in a maximum-security prison.'

'Kerry, the law with regards to Janice is clear. I know it's not a great situation but right now there are no other options,' Brendan replied patiently.

'Well, I've been thinking about that,' I said. 'What if you and I approach the judge and ask him to release Janice and tack her three-month sentence onto mine. I'll gladly take one for the team. She shouldn't even –'

'Kerry,' he cut in, smiling wryly at my gesture. 'Come on. It'll never happen.'

He was right, of course. Besides, I was about to find out I'd underestimated just how long my own sentence would end up being.

21

JUSTICE IS SERVED

Christmas Day 2003 would be the last time I'd speak to my mother. She'd suffered a head injury some years earlier and experienced continuing short-term memory loss. I rang Cheryl in the morning and she said she'd explained to Mum a few days earlier that I was in prison. She said Mum had blamed herself.

I hadn't spoken to my mother for well over a year and so I was surprised when Cheryl mentioned she was standing beside her and wanted to have a chat. When she got on the phone she said she hoped she'd see me for dinner later that night in Mildura. 'Chances are highly unlikely, Mum,' I said, and with that she wished me a Merry Christmas and said she hoped she'd see me in the coming days. She had blissfully returned to her vacant memory and was thankfully unaware that she was talking to her littlest girl from inside a prison on Christmas Day. As I hung up the phone, I felt a lifetime of resentment drain from my body, and for the first time in my life I thought, 'Poor Mum.'

She died in June the following year. Because I was a maximum-security prisoner I was not supposed to be allowed to attend her funeral in Mildura, but Brendan Money started pulling all the levers he could in order to get me to go anyway. I also had the support of five Corrections Officers who volunteered to take me up there on their own time. Although I cringed at the thought of being handcuffed at the funeral, my sister Cheryl promised that all of my siblings would wear handcuffs too so I wouldn't feel so out of place. After a couple of days, the path for me to be able to go was clearing: I had an officer willing to escort me, an overnight spot in the Mildura Holding Cells waiting for me, and a family willing to shackle their arms to protect my dignity. I was awfully humbled and grateful but in the end I said, 'No thanks. I'd rather not.' While people might have struggled to understand, they needn't have – I felt our last phone call had been goodbye enough.

That weekend, as Mum was given a private graveside send-off so she could reunite with Dad somewhere beyond the clouds, I wondered if my girls would ever be able to forgive me for leaving them. After all, it was more than a year that we'd been apart. At least my day of reckoning was nearly upon me and I looked forward to getting out soon and starting to repair the damage.

In all the time I'd been on remand I had made at least fifteen trips into the subterranean city so that my case could be mentioned before the courts. I was also subject to five adjournments until I finally sat in the dock to face the music. By the time the case was ready to be heard by a judge, the Crown alleged I'd stolen nearly $2 million between 1997 and 2003. Even though I could hardly comprehend the figure and it had increased exponentially during my incarceration, I pleaded guilty to the lot – four counts of theft and one count of obtaining property by deception. All told it accounted for $1,962,602 over six-and-a-half years. I had plundered the account of my employer and also defrauded my girls' daycare centre, where I had been a director. I had dipped into that business's books in a desperate bid to balance the account at the logging firm and cover my tracks as I strayed further and further from ever being able to pay any of the money back.

For legal reasons I can't and won't go into why my own estimation of what I'd stolen was closer to $500,000, but it doesn't matter anyway. I had frittered away other people's money on indulgences, on making my life appear better than it was and on pleasing myself and others. I wasted it on trinkets and toys, trips and food, and even gambled it away, although I was no more a gambler than I was a drug addict. In the end I simply had no regard for the money – something I was as ashamed of then as I am today. Yes, I was guilty and I would gladly accept whatever punishment society imposed upon me.

In October 2004 I was told to stand in the dock in the County Court of Victoria to be sentenced. Although Judge Betty King noted I had suffered sexual abuse as a teenager and endured extreme challenges during my twelve-year marriage, she said she had to balance my background, my guilty plea and my expressions of remorse 'against the great harm and damage done to so many other members of the community'. In declaring my fate Judge King adopted a decidedly bitter tone and kept referring to my 'superior intellect'. I sat there thinking, 'I'm not that smart, lady! Look where I am.' Yet she said there were no circumstances that mitigated my behaviour: I wasn't on drugs, I had no mental health issues, I wasn't an alcoholic, I wasn't a gambler. I had no excuses, so I must have been a criminal mastermind. Before I'd gone into court Paul Galbally had told me, 'Whatever you do, don't count the years, Kerry. Don't add it all up.' But when Judge King started to read out the penalty, counting was all I could do. She seemed to go on forever: two years for this, two years for that to be served concurrently with two years here and another consecutive two years there . . . I lost count at around fourteen years. The girls were going to be in their twenties by the time I got out.

I didn't have long to sit there and let it sink in. Two Corrections Officers quickly escorted me to the lift, whisking me back underground and out of the sight of Judge Betty King and the other upstanding members of society. One of the officers worked at the prison and they were both very gentle and sympathetic to me, but when the lift doors slid closed one of them looked at me and said, 'Well, it looks like you're in a bit of trouble.'

'Really? Ya think?' I said. 'Seriously, here I am in handcuffs between you two idiots and I'm about to go back to a maximum-security prison for God knows how long – and that's the best you can do?'

I was taken into an underground office where I was joined by a concerned-looking Paul Galbally five minutes later. 'You counted it all up, didn't you?' he said.

'Yeah,' I replied, 'but I got lost somewhere between fourteen years and life. So what's the sentence really?'

'Seven years with a non-parole period of four-and-a-half years,' he said. 'You've already served eighteen months so you'll be out in three more years – in late 2007.'

Suddenly my eyes filled with tears and, for one of the few times since the whole nightmare had begun, I felt them slip down my cheeks in the presence of another person. Paul looked at me with pity written across his face. 'Oh, Paul, it's not because of the sentence,' I said between sobs. 'I don't mind going back to prison. I'm just sad because I won't be seeing you again. I know that this is the end of the line for us and I'm going to miss you. You've been so good to me.'

'Kerry, we can appeal, you know,' he said. 'But I'm not sure – you might get twelve months off, you might get six months. You might not get anything.'

'You've done enough for me for nothing,' I said. 'You came along for the ride and there's no way I can ask you to spend more of your time and money to appeal against something that I'm guilty of. I don't want to appeal. I pleaded guilty and I vowed to accept whatever penalty the court handed down. I'm just grateful for everything you've done.'

When he left I never saw him again.

That night as I sat in the Brawler on the way home I reflected on my punishment. Although I received a longer sentence than some people did for killing an abusive husband, I was oddly OK with it. In fact, I was anxious to get back to DPFC where I knew people would have already heard about my fate. It was all over the TV and radio news. For a fraud case, I was given a lot of media attention. And for some reason the press went out of its way to refer to me as a 'mother of two'. Funny how they never mention children when men are sentenced. Back in the cottage the girls said they were shocked and dismayed at my extra three years, but I suspect they were also a little bit relieved. They liked having me around, and if I was honest, I liked having me around, too.

22

MASTER OF ARTS

It's ironic that I had to go to prison in order to get a university education. Tertiary study had never entered my mind as a youngster because it simply wasn't one of the cop-nurse-wife options Robinvale offered. Despite my turbo-charged high school education, I had been quite happy to let the academic wheels fall off. During one maths exam in year eleven I simply filled in my name and walked straight out of the classroom. I just didn't fit in and had grown tired of being around older kids who didn't like me. It was a shame because, as my family was always at pains to point out, 'You could be anything you want, Kerry.' Up until my final year I had always got excellent results right throughout school – except in English.

The problem was that I refused to read a book I didn't like, so when it came time to study literature I was always looking for a shortcut. Same when it came to writing. When I was in year three our teacher, Mr Thurgate, told us to compose a poem. I was absolutely dreading the assignment and spent the day pondering how to hand in a poem without actually writing one. That afternoon I went home and looked through our meagre library of books where I found a faded, ancient-looking tome titled *The Collected Works of . . .* some old man or other. I plunged deep into its yellowed pages until I found an obscure-sounding poem called *The Pied Piper of Hamelin.* 'Sounds like something a kid might say,' I thought, and set about transcribing it into my English book.

> *Hamelin Town's in Brunswick,*
> *By famous Hanover city,*
> *The river Weser, deep and wide,*
> *Washes its wall on the southern side,*
> *A pleasanter spot you never spied,*
> *But, when begins my ditty,*
> *Almost five hundred years ago,*
> *To see the townsfolk suffer so*
> *From vermin, was a pity . . .*

I handed it in the following day. Being all of nine years old it never occurred to me that Mr Thurgate would twig to the fact I had never been to Hamelin, Brunswick or Hanover. Nor did I think he would have been familiar with the work of the nineteenth-century English poet Robert Browning. After all, that book I found the 'ditty' in was really, really old. I honestly thought Mr Thurgate was going to be mightily impressed with my flair for the written word. Top marks were almost guaranteed.

'Kerry, would you please stand up in front of the class and read your poem aloud for everyone to hear?' he asked and waved me towards him. Wow. He must *really* be impressed, I thought.

'Hamelin Town's in Brunswick,' I began earnestly, 'By famous Hanover city . . .'

As soon as I finished my recital Mr Thurgate stepped over to me and snatched the poem from my hand. 'You little cheat,' he snapped. 'How dare you claim someone else's words as your own! It's as good as stealing!' Even though the humiliation I copped in front of the whole class made me reflect on what I had done, I don't think I went to confession that weekend and said, 'Forgive me, Father, for I stole a poem from Robert Browning.' I did, however, refrain from cheating on schoolwork from that day on. Still, I could be pretty unprepared when it came to English. At high school, plenty of kids were thrilled when we were told we'd be studying *The Hobbit*. Not me: I found Tolkien's Middle Earth to be a stuffy, up-itself place brimming with annoying, verbose creatures and the story itself threaded with silly plotlines. I stalled a quarter of the way through it and instead asked a classmate to sit down and explain to me what happened in the rest of the book. Unsurprisingly, I failed miserably.

There would be no such hijinks while studying writing inside DPFC. That's not because if I cheated a note would be sent home or I'd have to face the principal. It would simply mean I'd blown an incredible opportunity to improve myself. I gave it everything I had.

There had never been a university program inside DPFC and the opening arose through a prisoner named Akiyo. She was already doing her Master of Arts in Writing through Swinburne University when she was jailed for fraud offences. 'Why can't I continue studying in here?' she asked. It was a fair enough question, and I took a close interest in the prison's response to it. When the authorities – in conjunction with Swinburne University – agreed that Akiyo could indeed continue her degree with the assistance of tutors, I was among a number of inmates who immediately put their hands up to apply to study the same course. I knew leaving prison with a Masters would be one of the best things I could do, and I knew I'd also make connections on the outside along the way. Of the non-criminal variety.

Despite my shameful history of plagiarism as a nine-year-old and my disdain of the classics, I had a knack for writing. I used to pen a lot of comical items for roasts, weddings, birthdays and any other occasion that called for it. I sometimes even wrote funny poems and performed them at parties for fun. Mr Thurgate would have been proud. So when the pilot program teaching a Master of Arts in Writing at DPFC was launched and I was accepted, I was confident I'd be able to cope with the workload.

I loved it in the prison's Education building. I was immediately drawn to the women who ran the unit because they talked about normal things, and when I wasn't up to my armpits in peer support work I spent a fair amount of time in Education. Before long I came to value, trust and totally adore Carolyn Beasley – the Swinburne University tutor who came into the prison to teach five of us every Friday.

Carolyn had a doctorate in writing and my first impression was that she was a meek and mild dork. I automatically felt protective of her. I didn't want Carolyn to be taken advantage of by a prisoner sidling up to her and trying to get her to bring stuff in for them. Very quickly, however, I discovered she was no dork – she was smart, witty, hilarious and the best listener I had ever met. We became friends and those precious hours between 9am and midday on a Friday were a conduit to the relative sanity of the outside world.

Unlike the other Masters students in funky, well-funded campuses around the country, we didn't have computers or access to the internet, so Carolyn would print out everything we needed and bring it in with her. As a result the tutoring was pretty hands-on and intense, and it quickly became clear Carolyn was one of those souls who really, *really* cared about other people. I was thinking about that one day when it struck me that she was the first and only civilian who got to know me not as Kerry the suburban mum from Healesville, but Kerry Tucker from maximum security, Criminal Registration Number 171435. She had absolutely no knowledge of who I used to be, only of who I was. For three years she never saw me in anything other than a white T-shirt and blue tracksuit pants. Yet she still liked me! I would get extremely excited when I knew I'd be seeing Carolyn and devastated on days she couldn't make it. She made me realise just how intellectually malnourished I'd become and how starved of intelligent conversation I was.

As challenging as it could sometimes be, I worked very hard to uphold the promise I made to myself when I was first arrested: 'Don't let the system change you. Do not become like everybody else.' It was easier said than done, and the biggest danger was winding up speaking like the other inmates. The penal system has its own strong dialect that can differ markedly from state to state. In fact, inmates have even gone to the trouble of compiling the *Dictionary of Victorian Prison Slang* that includes helpful terms like:

Bronze-up: *vb* A form of protest involving smearing the walls of a cell with excreta.

And then there are the terms that are used in certain prisons around Australia. At that time in the DPFC women were forever saying, 'Sweeeeeet' as an affirmative response to inquiry. It drove me nuts.

'Here, Shaz, do you wanna finish off me Coke? I can't drink the rest.'

Shaz: '*Sweeeeeet.*'

You could substitute 'sweeeeet' with 'grouse', though it was pronounced 'grouw-w-w-w-s-e'.

'I'm making a brew, Shaz. Do you want one?'

Shaz: 'That'd be grouw-w-w-w-s-e, mate.'

I made damned sure whenever I was offering a hot beverage I would ask the girls if they wanted 'tea or coffee' as my internal voice reminded me, 'Don't say brew. Don't say brew . . .'

'Oh, I'd love a brew, Kerry. Ta.'

'No worries,' I'd say. 'Coming right up.' ('Don't say sweet. Don't say sweet . . .')

Nevertheless on any given day there were countless times I would have to adopt different dialects, depending on who I was speaking to. A lot of the women communicated in the sad, street-weary tongue of the uneducated, the unloved and the down-trodden. Whenever they needed me, I would speak to them in a way that made *them* feel at home, not me. I would gladly start droppin' me gees, flattenin' me vowels and sayin' 'seen' instead of 'saw', and 'done' instead of 'did'. Fucken anythin' to help make 'em feel safe 'n' protected, eh? Nobody wants to hear from Mrs McGillicuddy the grammar Nazi when they're hanging out.

When Carolyn arrived each week with her armful of papers and head full of interesting ideas it was like breathing in some fresh mountain air. We'd natter for hours and she was as eager to teach as I was to learn. Being denied the internet was just one of the challenges inmate students faced. We had to do everything with one week's turnaround because we weren't allowed to keep a huge amount of paper in our cells with us in case it caught fire. It was a hell of a way to make sure I got my homework done. If it wasn't completed before the next Friday rolled around the opportunity was gone as the curriculum just moved along.

The Master of Arts was a three-year course and it took the prison about a year to realise that we were going to be able to do it. There had been a view among some people that we were destined to fail but there we were, managing the workload and achieving good results. It was a lot of work but it was course work, that was the beauty of it; we didn't have to do exams. All of our assessments were major assessments of 5000 to 10,000 words but they made up the same marks and were subjected to the same scrutiny as exams.

One day our prayers were answered when the five of us students were given computers, courtesy of Swinburne University, which by then was quite keen on the trial prison project. It wasn't just a matter of Carolyn driving out with a van full of computers and backing up to the Education building: the machines sat at security for a month while the sniffer dogs went over them and the prison replaced the hard drives to make sure we only had access to Microsoft Word. When they finally installed the PCs in our cells I felt like all my Christmases had come at once. We had disks we could save our uni work onto and then take those disks to Education with us. But there was nothing stopping us using Word to write anything we wanted. At that point my journal writing really took off, but the thing having a computer helped most with was what I called my 'office work' – writing parole letters, applications and appeals for the other inmates. I even learned a little bit of Japanese so I could help Akiyo with her appeal. We sat with each other for hours preparing her case, which paid off when her sentence was reduced.

As a gesture of thanks Akiyo drew by hand two beautiful Japanese symbols and gave them to me. 'I can't give you anything other than this,' she said.

'Oh, thank you,' I replied. 'Tell me, what do they mean?'

Akiyo stood close beside me and pointed at her handi-work. 'This one is for mother,' she said quietly, 'and this one is for daughter.'

23

A MOTHER'S DAUGHTER

Some poor souls never really had a chance, right from the day they were born. They were the girls who left the biggest impressions on me: the ones who I'd sometimes lie awake at night and think about. One such soul was a pretty, intelligent and severely damaged girl in her early twenties who wound up in DPFC on drugs charges. I will never forget the day I received her as a terrified first-timer: she was sprawled haphazardly on a couch in A5 bawling her eyes out as she watched a TV news report.

'Hello, sweetie, I'm Kerry,' I said, crouching down next to her. 'Are you OK? Why don't you tell me what's upsetting you?'

She pointed weakly at the TV and sobbed, 'He killed my mum. No one cares about her because she was just a fucken hooker. No one cared then and no one cares now. No one gives a shit about any of us.'

'Well, I care, sweetheart,' I said. 'I honestly do.'

This poor girl was already terrified about being in prison but she grew increasingly upset about her forgotten mother to the point of hysteria. It seemed there was nothing I could say or do to console her. That night after lock-down, she tried to get the attention of the prison psychiatrists but she was told she had to wait in line – maybe next week. Instead, she turned to her old habits for comfort and smoked some marijuana, only to get caught and put in the slot the next morning.

As soon as I could I went down there to see her for an hour and assured her I would do everything to get one of the psych workers to see her. If she couldn't go to the mountain, I'd bring the mountain to her. I went straight to the Programs building and convinced them that the girl needed help now, not in a week's time. The psychiatrist on duty went directly to her and started the process that should have commenced ten years earlier. Unsurprisingly she was a walking almanac of psychiatric problems and was quickly transferred to the Special Needs Unit situated near the Protection building. It's off limits to everyone who isn't living there, and is full of schizophrenics, border-line personalities, people with severe mental health issues and self-harmers. As every repressed feeling spewed forth as though she was an emotional Krakatoa, she became hyper-aggressive and hard to handle. Although she was in Special Needs she was still in prison and that kind of behaviour would not be tolerated for long. Then she took a swing at another inmate and was promptly returned to the slot.

After two weeks in Isolation she was no longer deemed a Special Needs case and instead re-located to A1 – the most unstable, hostile and dead-end unit full of women no other inmate wants to live with. These were hard-core crims; the unforgiving types who knew every trick in the book and who wouldn't hesitate to assault anyone who pissed them off. She all but mentally drowned in that unit, but after a while she was transferred to Tarrengower, the minimum-security prison farm near Bendigo where inmates are sent ahead of their release. I was relieved because I thought it would be good for her. Four days after she was set free she died of an overdose.

Although death was becoming a commonplace occurence in my life, I let the ghosts of the departed roam around in my head. As bad as I am with names, I remembered all of theirs; each of the women I greeted with kindness and friendship and later waved goodbye to at the front gate. They all left a little piece of themselves under my skin. I can almost feel them – even today – and I will never, ever forget them.

When I first began receiving girls at Reception I could be left genuinely traumatised by what they told me, but after years of hearing the worst of what humanity has to offer I started to develop a thick scar tissue on my emotions. What had once been repellent became benign. This was pointed out to me one day when I was called down to help settle a girl who had been brought in on a murder charge. She had stabbed her partner more than twenty times and was more than happy to talk about it as I checked her out for injuries, signs of mental distress and drug issues.

'He came at me really fast so I just stabbed him right in the chest – twice!' the newbie said, reliving the horrific moment for me.

'Uh huh,' I said kind of absently as I scanned her hands and arms.

'Then he sort of fell back and I stabbed him in the neck.'

'Riiight . . .'

'And then I stuck the knife in his neck again and it made a really big hole and I could hear the air rushing in and out . . .'

'I see,' I said. 'Sweetie, would you like a tea or coffee? I can get you one if you like?'

'No thanks,' she said.

'OK, now – you were saying you stabbed him in the throat and you could hear a kind of whistling noise, is that right?'

Afterwards the officer who'd been standing outside the holding cell said, 'Kerry, do you think it's time you got a little bit of counselling yourself?'

'What do you mean?' I asked, surprised by the question.

'That story was fucking horrific and you're sitting there carrying on like she was talking about the weather!'

But the fact was I didn't need counselling. The girl did. And anyway, I'd heard more than a dozen stories that were just as bad as that and I never developed PTSD or even lost sleep. I just got up and got on with it. I was able to switch off and just disappear into the latest *Harry Potter* book or my uni work. And there was always another extreme event just around the corner that would soon occupy my thoughts.

24

VIOLENCE

For the most part, female prisoners are nowhere near as violent as their male counterparts. While murder, bashings and rioting are tools of the trade inside the men's prisons the 'fairer sex' is less likely to resolve problems with a swinging fist or at the end of a homemade knife. Women behind bars prefer to practise emotional thuggery – it's less messy, easier to conceal and it can be just as devastating as a vicious blow to the head. Fear, I also realised early on, can cut almost as deep as any blade.

If a woman had failed to pay a drug debt women would go to her cell window and issue all manner of threats: 'We're gunna get ya. You're fucken dead meat. The minute you go to Medical we're gunna beat the shit outta ya.' The poor girl on the receiving end would nearly go insane with fear. I'd never forgotten how such a mental assault had caused Miss Crime Family to try to hang herself in the Moorabbin cells a couple of years earlier and I can only imagine how someone like the suicidal newbie Sharon would have reacted to sustained verbal threats against her safety. She might have sawed right through her arms.

I was also very cognisant of the fact that quite a few of the murderers inside DPFC hadn't laid so much as a finger on another soul: they'd just convinced another person – usually a man – to kill for them. This sort of brainwashing took time – women could spend months and even years priming a third party to carry out the most unspeakable deeds so they didn't have to get their hands dirty. These were individuals with a capacity for long-range evil, which could be a concern in prison where vendettas stewed in a seemingly endless supply of time. I spent a good deal of my days trying to quietly unpick these tangled webs of perceived wrongs and bitter reprisals.

Sometimes, when I got wind that a woman was in danger of being bashed, I would calmly and discreetly approach the aggressor and appeal to her sense of decency and reason. 'I know you,' I would say. 'You've been here eighteen times since I've been here. I know you've had the crap beaten out of you by some piece of shit guy that you keep going back to. And now you're going to physically attack someone else? You're going to pay it forward? Honestly, what's your story?'

Often they'd sit there with no comeback other than, 'Oh, yeah. Look, I know, but I'm trying to get in with this other crew.'

'Well, that crew is going to fuck you over, sweetheart. They don't give a shit about you. And if you hurt another person, karma says that hurt will ultimately come back to you. So you need to think about it, OK?'

'Whatever.'

After a few years of pushing this message behind the scenes women started to work it out. 'Don't hurt each other. Be polite to the officers. Don't listen to your dipshit guy. We have to look out for each other in here. We've all suffered the same.' Of course it wasn't all kumbaya on the compound: women still had to go to Protection for trans-gressions like lagging on other prisoners or because of some major problem – perceived or real – between inmates. The person who was responsible for more women going into Protection during my time was Emma Kate – one of the most feared prisoners in Victoria.

Emma was a young, attractive and completely wild woman who was serving a fourteen-year term for murder. I don't want to detail Emma's history as it was a long time ago and everyone should have the opportunity to move on. Besides, I liked Emma. She would come to my cell with little presents of sparkling body wash to thank me for helping her type up notes for courses she was doing by correspondence. She would tell me how she wanted to have children when she got out, and we often talked about my girls and what it's like to be a mum.

Unfortunately there was a constant flow of women coming in and out of the prison who had history with her. Nevertheless I knew I could trust Emma's word if she said it was all fine between her and, say, Josephine. If she said, 'Nup, and I'm gunna fucken kill her,' then I'd go to Josephine and advise her that she needed to ask for Protection. It was a mark of how much responsibility I had and how much faith the administration placed in me – they always knew I'd guide Josephine to that decision for her own safety. I managed to straddle that line between 'us and them', and since it was always for the better, no one minded. The women trusted me and I trusted them. None of them ever promised me a rival was going to be safe and then ended up killing them.

Sometimes Brendan Money or one of the governors would come to me with information. 'Gemma is coming back in and we know about the drug issues,' a governor told me once. 'She owes a debt to Janet, right?'

'So I believe.'

'OK, can you make some inquiries and find out the best place for us to place Gemma?'

So off I went to have a chat with Janet. Normally I kicked these delicate discussions off with, 'Do you want a cigarette?'

Janet: '*Sweeeet.*'

As soon as I mentioned the fact Gemma was coming back in, Janet flew into a rage. 'She's fucken done for, Kerry. I'm gonna knock her fucken head off, right?'

'OK, Janet, we have to come to some kind of agreement here,' I said, plonking myself on the bench beside her. 'If you go attacking Gemma it's going to affect your parole. I'm the one who's going to write your letter and the prison will make me list any offences you've racked up. You're on shaky ground already but I really, *really* want you to have the best chance of getting out next time, OK? I need you to be honest with me: are you really going to bash Gemma? I need to know because I don't want to see you in more trouble.'

'Nah, I'm not gonna bash her,' Janet said. 'But she's gotta pay her fucken debts.'

With Janet onside I was then able to go to the rest of her crew and pave the way for Gemma to come back in without any reprisal. To make sure Gemma was totally safe, I asked people from other crews to keep a covert eye on her and let me know if there were any signs of trouble. It was a fascinating part of my job – I called it 'chess with murderers'.

With 300 pawns on the board – many of them desperate and inclined to lashing out – outbursts of violence were inevitable. It might have been a last resort, but when women did it, they did it big. The only place in DPFC that wasn't under constant video surveillance was the ironically named 'Leisure Centre', a glorified and ill-equipped gymnasium. It was amazing to me that the prison could monitor women at all times but when they were working out – and had access to barbells and a pool table – that was considered an invasion of privacy. Inevitably, the gym was a danger zone for anyone who had seriously transgressed the prison code.

One day I got wind that an attack was imminent but the details were so hush-hush I didn't even know who was involved. The very next day a girl was savagely beaten inside the Leisure Centre. The assailants placed pool balls inside a sock and swung it at her head until it was cracked open. That woman is now permanently scarred. The person who was behind it wound up being charged and put in the slot for eight months for good measure. She was an ally of mine – a senior crim who I had a lot of dealings with in regards to prison strategies. I liked her and we got along well. She finally got out after eighteen years only to die shortly afterwards from a heart attack. She'd only texted me the night before.

When I arrived at DPFC, thirty-eight out of the forty beds in the Protection Unit were full. When I left, only two people remained in there. It had been a matter of changing the old-school code of reprisal. 'Get your own shit right. If it's got nothing to do with your sentence, then butt out.' Slowly but surely, it started to change. At the beginning I would encourage girls to take part in prison rehab programs only to be told, 'I'm never going to do it. I'm never going to change.' Still, I kept it up and four years later a fifty-five-year-old woman, who'd been on drugs for the better part of forty-four years, approached me. 'Kerry, I just went to the program for the first time and I don't think I'm going to do drugs again. I'm going to give it my best shot and while I may fail tomorrow, I'm gonna keep trying, right?'

'It's all we can do, sweetie,' I'd say. 'Just keep trying.' I really liked Annie.

That was a bit rich coming from me, though. I'd manage to gain a Masters Degree but fail the anger management program four times.

25

KILLER COMPANY

Although the women I lived with at the cottage were responsible for killing no fewer than five people between them, we all got on quite well. One of them, a forty-year-old chronic alcoholic named Wendy, had actually killed two people – young sisters – when she crashed her car into theirs in Chirnside Park. Wendy had fifty-five drink-driving charges against her, was unlicensed, driving an un-roadworthy and unregistered car and was blind drunk when she careened into the girls as they were driving home from a shift at McDonald's. Wendy got six years with a non-parole period of four. She had wiped two young lives from the face of the earth . . . and yet she received a shorter prison sentence than me. Go figure. The community was outraged, however, and the prosecutor appealed, so in the end she got eight years with a non-parole period of six.

Although we were both peer support workers, Wendy treated me like a princess, no matter what I said to her. If I lost patience and snapped at her she didn't seem to mind. She would constantly talk about how no one cared about *her* kids. 'Well that's right, Wendy,' I would say, 'they don't. You've got to understand that that's because you're responsible for taking another family's children off them forever.'

Still, I generally got along well with her in prison and enjoyed her company. Quite often there's a marked difference in the person a woman is in prison from the one she is on the outside.

Sue was a very calm and quiet woman who we were blessed to have in the unit because she was an excellent cook. A great lover of ballroom dancing, Sue was dubbed 'The Dancing Assassin' after she was convicted of murdering her husband. She'd convinced another man to kill for her, hoping to cash in on her husband's demise. Unfortunately she discovered he had written her out of his will. Worse, the bumbling hit man she'd found had attempted to make the death look like a suicide but the victim's body was found floating next to his car in a reservoir near Castlemaine. Very few people take their lives by drowning, and forensics later found haemorrhages behind his eyes consistent with strangulation.

Like Wendy, Sue treated me well, and although few people liked her I got on with her for the most part. She was forever sitting and quietly knitting, but she was always listening to what was going on and she never dropped a stitch. She was like a smiling, sitting, knitting, dancing assassin who took it all in and filed it away to be used in some later campaign to her advantage. She endured the pain of seeing her family grow in her absence, and became a proud but heartbroken grandmother behind bars.

One of the loveliest killers I ever met was Jo. I lived with her for quite a while in the unit. She was a tiny, bird-like woman who possessed one of the most gorgeous natures of any inmate I got to know inside DPFC. She loved anything that grew: the grass, flowers – even the Deer Park weeds. She was jailed for killing her lesbian lover with a single, fateful thrust of a knife. Apparently Jo's girlfriend was a much bigger woman and one night they started fighting in their kitchen. During the scuffle Jo grabbed a knife off the bench and lashed out at her lover, striking her in the chest. After I got to know Jo I came to believe she did indeed act in self-defence because she literally would not hurt a fly – she'd try to usher them out of the cottage instead. But presented with a bloodied knife, a stab wound and a dead lover, the police charged her with murder.

One day a woman from a Christian church came out to speak to Jo. At the time she was working with lawyers to have her charge downgraded to manslaughter on the basis she acted in self-defence. Jo hadn't entered a plea at that point and so the lady from the church saw an opportunity to do God's work. She told Jo the only way she could save herself from eternal damnation was if she repented in the eyes of the Lord. 'You must confess before the Almighty! Thou shalt not kill! It is a sin! Repent, repent, repent!' It had been one hell of a fire-and-brimstone performance because she convinced Jo to plead guilty to murder. As soon as she came back to the cottage and told us I went ballistic. I marched straight to the Visitor Centre and grabbed hold of Sister Sue Idiot. 'Who do you think you are, to play God with people's lives?' I snarled. 'I'll make sure you never set foot inside this prison again.'

I left her standing there, mouth agape, and went straight to the governor: 'You need to get that woman out of here permanently,' I said, 'because if you don't I'm going to put it out on the compound and let everyone know that she almost got Jo sentenced to life. Not even Jesus would be able to save her after that.' The governor was appalled and agreed wholeheartedly, and Sister Sue Idiot was advised her service was not further required at DPFC and told to never return.

I had nothing against people ministering to inmates and have always thought one's personal religious beliefs are sacred and to be respected, but I did have a problem with anyone who sought to use some higher power to influence how a woman should plead. Fortunately it was a position that had the full support of the DPFC inmates and management alike. A few days later I ran into Brendan Money on the compound. 'So, I hear you're going after nuns now, Kerry,' he said with a smile.

'She asked for it,' I replied.

After dodging that bullet from heaven, the prosecution agreed to downgrade Jo's charge to manslaughter. She pleaded guilty and was sentenced to four years non-parole. That was half a year shorter than my non-parole period. Go figure again.

Perhaps the trickiest roommate I had was a stocky bottle-blonde woman named Jodi, but I will always think of her as 'Dolphin Girl'. She killed her partner by strangling him with curtain wire before stringing him up to a tree branch so everyone would think he'd hanged himself. Jodi was powerfully built with fingers like sausages, but she had the mental capacity of a twelve-year-old girl. This explained how she was able to hoist a man's body up a tree by herself – and also how she could think anyone would be convinced it was suicide.

Like Janice before her, Jodi seemed to feel safe around me and that's partly why she'd been put into our unit; so I could babysit her. It was the last thing I needed, but, just like everyone else in there, she was a lost and trampled soul and I felt compelled to help her in any way I could. The problem was that not everyone was as patient with her as me. It could make things tricky. Sue didn't care for her at all so whenever she went for Jodi, I'd go for Sue. Like Janice, I thought Jodi had no place being locked up in an adult prison. As much as she annoyed me from sun-up until sun-down she'd then say something like 'I wish I was like you, Kerry', and my heart would melt and I'd think about making her a cup of tea.

Sometimes, though, my patience would run out. I walked in after a particularly challenging day on the compound to find Jodi going off her head at the TV. There had been a report on the news about a dead dolphin with stab wounds that had washed up on the coast. 'Oh my God! OH MY GOD! They killed a dolphin!' Jodi wailed. 'What sort of person would do such a thing to a poor, defenceless little dolphin? What would a dolphin ever do to make someone stab it? Oh my God!'

She was starting to hyperventilate and get extremely agitated when I decided enough was enough. 'What in the fuck are you carrying on like that for?' I sniped. 'It's a fucking fish! You killed a man with curtain wire, for Christ's sake!' I took a breath and was about to offer Jodi some more advice on not being such an idiot about the stupid bloody dolphin when I caught sight of the other girls looking at me in alarm. Some were making the silent slitting gesture across their throats in a clear sign for me to knock it off. Jodi stormed off to her cell in tears.

'Kerry,' someone said, 'have you looked at her wall lately?'

I walked down to Jodi's cell, pushed the door open and found her sobbing on the bed while the smiling eyes of several dozen dolphins looked down on her from photos she'd cut out of newspapers and magazines and stuck on the walls.

'Oh.'

Jodi was freed after three years. I didn't resent the fact these killers were doing shorter sentences than me at all – each woman's case was her own business. No one else knew what it was like to walk a mile in their shoes. Besides, soon I would have a real friend to hang out with.

26

BABES BEHIND BARS

The DPFC was an endless series of hard surfaces and dull tones. What little carpet it had was paper thin, all the benches were hard, the concrete walls were hard, the paths and the grass were hard and even the women were hard. All this architectural and emotional brutalism was daubed in barren shades of beige, grey and dark blue – everything except the children's play equipment that is.

Under Victorian law, a mother who is serving a custodial sentence in a maximum-security prison is permitted to care for a child under the age of five inside the prison, in circumstances where there hasn't been either a violent crime or a child-related crime committed by the mother. Sometimes children are born to a mother in prison; other times the mother of a child will apply to bring them in if they're living in the community. The children must be kept with their mother at all times under a strict regime that forbids fighting or any dirty urines. Mothers are extra regularly and randomly urine-tested to ensure they are free of drugs, and this is overseen and supported by the Parenting Program within the prison. If the mother gets sick, an approved carer is appointed and is the only other person the child can be left with. The carer must also be drug free, of good conduct and well known to the child.

Obviously if a woman is pregnant when she's brought in and gives birth while she's incarcerated (children are delivered at a hospital, not in the prison), then the baby will stay with her in most cases until she's released or the child is four, going on five. The child must leave by the age of five so that they are ready for school in the community. Tragically the majority of the babies born to women at DPFC came into the world as tiny, howling heroin addicts. The mothers would be brought back into the prison while the poor bubs remained in hospital until they had withdrawn. Only then were they reunited behind the razor wire.

Other women who already had children on the outside were allowed to bring them into the prison to live permanently with them rather than face the prospect of long-term separation or foster care.

While the average taxpayer might reel at the thought of young kids being locked away behind a six-metre-high prison fence, I will go to my grave believing it is the best policy for both mother and child. In too many instances – like the cross-generational child-rape night-mare inflicted on people like Tara and her daughter – the alternatives can be beyond horrifying. At least in prison the child is with their mother who is surrounded by other women and has access to myriad support programs to help her look after them. And unlike the cruel world on the other side of the fence, there was never a time in DPFC when a child was in any danger whatsoever – there were literally hundreds of women to protect them.

Children softened the prison in the most beautiful and palpable ways. Even the hardest of surfaces yield a little when they reflect the chiming, melodious sounds of little people at play. Sharp edges were knocked off the inmates, too. Women would gather around just to watch the children gambol on the grassed areas near the cottages, and I noticed they shelved their foul language and became the sweetest versions of themselves. There was no fighting or raised voices, just ladies – many of them mums themselves – happy to revel in the innocence of childhood.

I pointed this out to Brendan Money. 'These children are having an amazing effect on the place,' I said. 'But they could really use some decent play equipment.' As always, he was already organising things.

Brendan Money was an excellent administrator who knew a good initiative when he saw one. Soon enough some funding was made available for some play equipment in bold shades of red, green, yellow and blue. It included a slippery dip, a tunnel, climbing frames and a sandpit, and was set up right next to the long-termers in the C area.

On a bleak, grey compound that had been devoid of colour for many years there suddenly stood a shining plastic citadel that gave the children a place to frolic and the inmates a place to dream of better days. And it was an enormous relief to hear women speak without swearing for once.

By watching court coverage in the media I had a pretty good grasp of the cases involving women in Victoria – particularly the high-profile ones. Over time I got to know which women were connected with particular criminal interests outside and inside DPFC. Putting the wrong person in the wrong unit could spell trouble and I would sometimes have to alert Brendan Money and the governors to potential flashpoints when it came to placements on the compound.

The same applied with high-profile cases involving women who were charged with a serious crime for the first time – because some were particularly vulnerable to being taken advantage of. I kept detailed computerised journals on who was coming and going. The minute I was called on to welcome a new arrival I was well prepared because I'd studied the form, their prior histories on previous sentences and their prison networks: 'This is who the girl is. This is where she lives. Here's what she's in for and this is what her nature is like, according to evidence reported in the media.'

Renate Mokbel and Tania Herman were two women who I did some homework on – mostly by paying attention to the media reports but also by reading the mood towards them among the other inmates. By my reckoning both of them were at risk in DPFC but for different reasons. At the time of her incarceration 'Melbourne mother of three' Renate Mokbel possessed one of the most infamous surnames in the country. Her brother-in-law, the notorious Melbourne drug lord Tony Mokbel, sat at the top of Australia's Most Wanted list alongside a whopping $1 million reward for information leading to his arrest. Tony had skipped bail and secretly fled the country in 2006. While that might have been good news for him, it spelled disaster for Renate who was jailed for failing to pay a $1 million surety for him.

When Renate arrived at the prison she was naturally considered a rock star of the criminal world – particularly among the drug users. Tony Mokbel was a marquee under-world name; a high-volume trafficker who was considered the last man standing in the brutal Melbourne drug wars that had claimed the lives of more than thirty people. As the most wanted man in the land, his face was plastered all through the media. Renate, however, was just a lovely suburban mum.

In the beginning I focused on finding a strategy that would allow her to settle in without becoming a target. The last thing a rock star needs in prison is groupies. I knew that everyone with even a whiff of a drug habit would try to befriend her and, pretty soon, they'd look for ways to stand over her and pressure her to get drugs into the prison. It took me about two minutes to deduce Renate was a complete clean-skin, just like me. In spite of her cocaine-laced surname, she had never once used drugs and – as far as I could see – she was merely a victim of having the wrong surname. Since Renate's mum was dying of cancer, this mostly left her teenage children struggling to look after their little brother, who was just two years old. Renate was a thoroughly delightful and disarming woman who could sometimes come off as a bit of an airhead, so I nicknamed her 'Bubbles'. We bonded straight away over our many shared interests – the biggest being a desperate longing for our kids. She, like me, cared for nothing else.

Renate was anxious to get her little boy in to live with her in the prison. For that to occur I needed to get her out of Remand and into the C Units as soon as possible. That would be seen as a privilege because you're supposed to pay your dues in A5 before ascending the pecking order, but as far as I was concerned I'd changed the culture enough that I didn't care about 'the code' anymore. I made an appointment to see Brendan Money and start the process. 'You know who Renate is and what she represents to a lot of the women in here,' I said. 'She's going to be much, much safer up in our unit than being at the mercy of A5. They'll rip her to shreds in record time. Everyone will want a piece of her, but I know she's got absolutely nothing for them. She's a complete and utter squarehead. She's one hundred per cent clueless and vulnerable in here. She doesn't need that kind of trouble right now and, frankly, neither does anyone else.'

He didn't disagree and after several weeks and a bit of to-ing and fro-ing, we arranged for Renate to move into the unit and squeeze into the double room with Wendy.

'Alright,' I said to Renate, 'step two is you've got to make yourself Brendan Money's best friend. You have to stop being so shy. He needs to see that you're strong enough to withstand anything that goes on around you; that you're smart enough, that you're savvy enough, friendly enough and an excellent mother who will have no trouble taking care of your son. He needs to see that in you and you need to start doing it now.'

Renate followed my instructions to a tee but the biggest obstacle to getting her son into the prison was the media. Her family name attracted so much press hatred and public mistrust that such a move would have been dressed up – wrongly – as 'Special Jail Privilege for the Mokbels!' There would have been a huge public outcry and the *Herald-Sun* would have campaigned to stop it happening. In the absence of the arch-villain Tony to sink their pens into, the media pack salivated over Renate's case, which brought the glare of publicity onto the prison, too. We had to wait four months until the journos had moved onto the next saga to arrange to have Renate's little boy brought into DPFC under the cover of darkness.

I became one of Renate's 'back-up mothers' in the event she fell ill and needed help looking after her boy. Having Renate with me made my prison life all the more bearable because we were so like-minded. We'd laugh at the same things and weep at the same things too. She would get off the phone from her older kids Jade and Robbie in tears, and I would get off the phone from Sarah and Shannyn in the same state. We became very close. Since we had both been dealt with by detectives from the Purana Taskforce, I even told her the story of how they had set off my vibrator while searching my room – something I swore I would never reveal to another soul as long as I lived. Bubbles thought it was hilarious.

Renate's boy blossomed in prison. He was a sweet, funny little man and although he had twigged that we weren't living in a normal house, he thought we were all 'at work'. He would write/scribble on some of the cards I sent to my girls because he realised that they couldn't come and visit me at work and he wanted to help. He had about thirty great aunties who treated him like a little prince. I can honestly say prison was the best place for him – right alonside his mother.

It was a bitterly cold day in June 2007 when news broke that Purana Taskforce detectives had arrested Australia's most wanted man, Tony Mokbel, in Greece. He had been posing as a local fisherman and wearing an absurd wig. The stupid-looking mug shot flashed around the country in breaking-news bulletins as Renate and her son were still asleep. 'Renate,' I whispered, trying not to wake the sleeping boy. 'I have to tell you something.'

'Hmm?' she said sleepily.

'They've found Tony. He's in Greece and he's wearing the most ridiculous-looking wig.'

It was a surreal moment when I truly wondered how I had gone from a quiet suburban life to being at the centre of such infamous events, but it certainly wasn't the first.

*

I was also quite fond of Tania Herman – another square-head newbie – who found herself thrown in with the lions at DPFC. Tania had been charged with the attempted murder of a Melbourne woman, Maria Korp, in what became known as the body-in-the-boot case. Tania was the mistress of Maria's husband, Joe Korp, who had hatched a plan to do away with his wife and live happily ever after with Tania. He convinced Tania to strangle Maria, but after Tania choked the woman unconscious she panicked and bundled her body into the boot of Maria's car, which she abandoned in Melbourne's Royal Botanic Gardens. Four days later Maria was found – still in the boot and barely clinging to life.

Joe and Tania were subsequently charged with attempted murder. Tania pleaded guilty but Joe maintained his innocence. After six months in a coma, Maria Korp's life support was turned off, but the charges were never upgraded to murder due to a deal prior to Maria's death. Nevertheless, Tania was eventually sentenced to twelve years in prison. I had been following the case in the media and knew Tania's situation was a delicate one. The other inmates weren't upset that she had attempted to kill another woman, but weren't happy that she had confessed to everything and thereby 'given Joe up' in the process.

I conferred with Brendan Money about her pending arrival. 'As far as the men's prison is concerned she's given Joe up so she's going to have to go to Protection,' he said.

I felt it was unreasonable that a woman who had confessed to the crime and taken the consequences on the chin was going to spend the next twelve years locked away from other human beings because of the daft 'code'. Some knucklehead in the men's prison had got word through to his girlfriend at DPFC that Tania was some kind of subhuman and I was supposed to respect that as word from on high? No way! Besides, just about every person in prison broke 'the code' whenever it suited them anyway.

'Can't you please let me work with her instead, Brendan?' I asked.

'Kerry, it'll be your worst nightmare, trying to keep her safe every day for years,' he cautioned.

'Just let me try and assimilate her into the compound, please?'

'OK, but at the first sign of problems you've got to let me know,' Brendan insisted. 'If it becomes an unsafe situation – I need to know. She cannot be at risk on the compound. I'm trusting you.'

No pressure! Although looking after Tania wasn't my 'worst nightmare', it certainly wasn't without its challenges. As I chaperoned her around the compound one woman yelled out, 'You're a dog, Herman! You're a rat, dog motherfu–'

'What the fuck has it got to do with you? It's not your sentence. It's not your business,' I bellowed back at her. By the time I felt comfortable speaking to prisoners like that I had already written five parole letters for them, looked after them while they were withdrawing and got them access visits with their kids. No one was going to challenge me directly, not because they were afraid of me but because they respected me.

I steadily changed the culture around Tania in the prison and she ended up doing her entire sentence on the compound. Some old-school crims tried to flex their muscles about it but I just kept telling them the code was crap. 'Some guy who has belted the crap out of you for your whole life – you're going to listen to him about the code? The men have got their own code and it's a dickhead's code. We're women, we're smarter. Tell me I'm not right.' Fewer and fewer people could. Over time DPFC became less of an animal house and more a place where people got their kids in, and did programs to better themselves. As strange as it sounds, the prison became quite a nice environment.

On the day of Maria Korp's funeral, her husband, Joe – who had been freed on bail – hanged himself inside his garage. It was huge news in Melbourne as the body-in-the-boot case had dominated headlines for months. Again, it fell to me to be the messenger. Tania was in Medical at the time and had no idea what had happened.

'Tania,' I said gently, 'there's something I need to tell you. Joe has committed suicide.'

I'm not at liberty to say what her response was.

27

LOST AND FOUND

For thousands of women arriving at DPFC, I was the first inmate they had any meaningful contact with. Ever conscious of this privileged responsibility, I focused on making them feel as safe and as reassured as possible. As the old saying goes, first impressions count. On the flipside, almost all of the women I welcomed left a first impression on *me*, ranging from warmth, pity, anger, disdain, affection or anything in between. Sometimes their personal impact left a kind of stain on me that I could never quite scrub off. Some women, however, left me with deep, permanent wounds that have been carved into my memory forever. Women like Nikki.

One morning in early 2006 I received a routine call to attend Reception. 'Kerry, can you take care of this girl please? She's going to be transferred to hospital later on but needs a bit of a walk and fresh air.'

Nikki was sitting in the monitored cell looking rather depressed and washed out. She was also wearing a long-sleeved jacket, which struck me as a little odd since it was a typical scorching day in sunny old Deer Park. 'Hello, sweetie,' I began gently, settling myself on the bed next to her. 'I'm Kerry and I'm here to look after you while you're here. I want you to know you don't have anything to worry about, OK?'

She nodded softly.

'I'm going to take you outside for a walk around now,' I continued. 'It's really quite hot out there, do you think you might want to take your jacket off?'

'Umm, no thanks.'

No sweat. I walked outside with her so she could stretch her legs, get some sun and maybe have a cigarette. After a little while we sat down together in the middle of the compound in the blistering heat of the day. 'What's going on, Nikki?' I pressed her gently. 'It's ridiculously hot out here, are you sure you won't feel better without your jacket on?'

As Nikki rearranged herself on the bench her sleeves pulled back a little and that's when I saw what she'd been trying to hide. There appeared to be two steel zippers running up her forearms. She knew I'd seen them and, a little reluctantly, revealed the whole horror show. From the base of each palm to the inside of each elbow there were about 100 staples clipped side by side into this poor creature's flesh. Clearly her arms had been sliced wide open. Now, these weren't the Officeworks staples you load into your desktop stapler – they were industrial-sized, medical-grade clips that were so big and shiny they glinted in the sunlight.

I had never seen anything like it and I was horrified, but any outward sign only lasted for a second or two because I didn't want this young woman to feel ashamed. First impressions count. So, two or three heartbeats after the urge to reel away from her pulsed through me, I re-took control. It was my job to protect her and at this moment that meant shielding her as best I could from any further emotional injury her ghastly wounds might inflict on her. I pretended her scars were no big deal to me; hell, I saw that sort of thing every day! In truth, however, they were ugly, vicious injuries that sent an icy chill through my blood. It was clear she hadn't been hurt by accident and it was also obvious the resulting wounds had the potential to put up a barrier between Nikki and other people. I was determined not to let that happen.

'Oh dear, are they sore?' I inquired, softly resting my hand on her wrist as I looked reassuringly into her face. I wanted her to know that the repellent sight in front of us wouldn't deter me from reaching out and touching her or talking to her about the reality. I was honouring the truth of whatever nightmare she'd been through. When my hand touched hers I felt the tension drain out of her a little.

'Yeah, they are a bit sore,' Nikki admitted quietly.

'Is there anything I can get you, or try to get you, to help them feel a little better?'

'Nah, I don't want anything,' she replied, letting her guard down a little more with each exchange. 'Just a friend.'

Well, look no further! Over the next little while, Nikki told me how she'd come to be so hideously wounded. She was in a tempestuous relationship with some crazed fuckwit of a boyfriend she was so fearful of that she some-times tried to run away. The guy was obviously a psycho because one day, as Nikki attempted to flee yet again, he pinned her hands against a wall and drove a knife through each palm like some sort of suburban DIY crucifixion. Then he started to skin her alive, but for some reason he didn't finish the job and stopped at her arms. Apparently it had been rather hard work.

The result of his half-hearted mutilation was three slices of skin on each arm were tied at Nikki's wrists. and at the elbows – hence the use of several hundred enormous staples to try to put her tattered limbs back together again.

'So, what on earth are you doing in here?' I wanted to know.

It turned out she had also attacked the boyfriend at some point, and the police had warrants out for her arrest. 'My God,' I thought to myself. 'What a twisted world we live in.' Although it had been a harrowing day with the poor girl with the butchered arms, I was pleased that I'd been able to reassure her and connect with her, emotionally and physically, and that she was also able to verbalise what had happened to her. I had a sense that it was of crucial impor-tance. I was also slightly surprised that the prison had actually trusted me to look after an actual human being again considering I'd lost the last one . . .

A day or so earlier the officers at the Medical Unit asked me to take another woman named Sophie for a walk and entertain her between lunch and afternoon muster because she, too, was only going to be with us for the day. Still, it was unfair to keep her cooped up inside Medical with no access to fresh air for the whole day so they called me – the trusted, responsible and on-the-ball peer educator!

I walked alongside this frightened, precious woman as I gave her the guided tour of DPFC. 'You've got nothing to worry about, Sophie,' I assured her as we sauntered among the murderers, robbers and violent long-termers. 'I'm with you and you'll be one hundred per cent safe.' Still, the poor thing's eyes were like dinner plates: after all, she was a complete newbie who was only in for shoplifting a couple of T-shirts! She was genuinely terrified and overwhelmed by where she was.

As we neared 'Movement Control' – the general office on the compound that handles the flow of inmates between the various units and other prisons – a group of women approached me, most upset that they were about to be transferred to the minimum-security prison at Tarrengower. They didn't want to go. 'What can we do about it, Kerry?' they pleaded. 'Can you please help us?'

Before I knew it I was shanghaied into the dispute to try to find a solution. Sometimes when DPFC is full, management opens up more beds by transferring people to Tarrengower, where women can also be sent for 'pre-release' in the final stages of their term. Because it's a minimum-security prison farm, the inmates must be on short sentences. The problem is that this messes with women's access visits as most relatives find it difficult to travel all the way to Bendigo. Tarrengower is also where the state's female child sex offenders are held, so overall it's not the most appealing option.

I told the women to calm down and said I'd try to sort things out. Negotiating a satisfactory end to the stand-off took the best part of an hour and only when we'd reached an understanding that suited everybody did I leave. I'd barely stepped back outside the office when I ran straight into Wendy from my unit. She'd also had a challenging day. 'I'd kill for a brew,' Wendy declared with a Hollywood roll of her eyes.

'You took the words right out of my mouth,' I replied. We wandered home together to the cottage where Wendy knocked up a nice coffee. About thirty minutes later I was sitting there contentedly basking in the afterglow of my little caffeine fix when a niggling voice started to pipe up from the far back paddocks of my subconscious. There was something that needed my attention but I couldn't quite put my finger on it. 'K-e-r-r-r-e-e-e-y,' the voice in my head kept calling from a distance, but I kept drawing a blank on what else it was I had to do. Oh well.

Wendy and I chatted for a while longer and I nodded sympathetically while she catalogued what a bastard of a day she'd been having. Then she changed the subject: 'Hey, did you see that new girl in Medical?'

Those words hit me like a bolt of lightning and I jolted out of my chair. *'New girl in Medical . . .'* The little voice in my head that had been trying to tell me about it was now bellowing 'FUCK! FUCK! FUCK! YOU FORGOT ABOUT THE GIRL!' I was in a full panic. I'd got so caught up in the dramas at Movement Control that I'd left Sophie out the front while I sorted things out – and now she'd gone! 'Shit!' I gave myself up to Wendy straight away and begged for her mercy and understanding, and for her to help me find Sophie. If I didn't locate her ASAP I'd be in the deepest shit of my prison life.

I could hardly believe what was happening: dire scenarios flashed through my mind as it dawned on me that I'd left a vulnerable and frightened woman somewhere in the middle of a maximum-security prison. She was only in on minor shoplifting charges, for Christ's sake! My reassuring words to her were now echoing inside my head: 'I'm with you and you'll be one hundred per cent safe.'

'Oh my God, where is she?'

Wendy and I agreed to split up and start searching.

'OK. Shit. Fuck! First thing – what does she look like?' Wendy asked.

'Well, ah, Wendy, you see that's the thing – she's a bottle blonde with four inches of black re-growth starting at the scalp, she's got no front teeth and she's very skinny,' I said. It was a fairly accurate description of every second prisoner in DPFC. 'Oh yeah, and she was last seen wearing a white T-shirt, blue tracksuit pants and prison-issue runners.' In other words, she was dressed exactly the same as the other 300 people there. A needle in a haystack.

On this day, I realised for the first time just how much women in prison look alike from behind. I hurried around the compound thinking I'd found my missing charge only to tap her on the shoulder and be looked at askance by someone else. Before long, Jenny Hayes the prison chaplain and Mr McKenzie, the A5 senior supervisor, were also onto it. But rather than freak out they appeared to enjoy my dilemma. After two long hours I came up empty-handed and realised with a sense of dread that my only option was to wait until last call for muster, stand out in the middle of the compound and wait until Little Miss Houdini was flushed out. Sophie would have no door to stand beside as each unit was shut down, therefore she'd be the only woman on the compound – other than me. And that's exactly how I 'found' her in the end.

It turned out that while I was fighting the battle in Movement Control, another group of women walked past and Sophie thought it was the same group I'd been in the middle of. After all, everyone looks the same. She followed along as the women went back to their unit, which happened to be the furthest one away from the compound. When they realised they'd picked up a stray they felt sorry for her and invited her in for coffee.

Since I knew Sophie didn't know anyone and that inmates tended not to be overly friendly to new arrivals, I didn't think to actually *go into* any of the units – I just scoured the front of each one on the compound instead, along with all fifty-two women in A5 just in case she'd wandered in there. I'd considered having her paged, too, but since she had no clue about the prison she'd have had no idea where to go if her name was called out. Also, paging her would have alerted Medical to the fact I'd actually lost their prisoner.

Thankfully, I returned Sophie to Medical at the required time, but by then it was already too late: the staff, like everyone else in the prison, was already onto it. 'Kerry Tucker lost a prisoner! Bah-ha-ha-ha!' Oh how they laughed. 'Inside a maximum-security prison, no less! A-ha-ha-haaaa!' I had to laugh too: it really had been quite an achievement to misplace a fully grown human being inside a prison that is specifically designed to know exactly where everybody is at all times.

So, I was slightly amazed that they trusted me with Nikki. She was a gentle soul and I could see relief in her eyes as she reached out to me for friendship and safety. I gave both to her – I'd have given her more if I could. I took her up to my unit and organised a care package to make her stay in Medical more comfortable: some Christmas cake, biscuits and red cordial. Nikki thought it was very special. I could always count on the women in my unit to provide my strays with little bags of goodies: I was forever bringing the walking wounded home with me – at least two a week – and the girls always sent them off with a little hamper.

These rudderless, lost and lonely little creatures broke my heart: the challenged girls, the girls with head injuries, the ones who clung to me like small children being left at school on their first day. The girls like Nikki. I've been told they appealed to the rescuer part of my self-destructive/ rescuer personality. I don't know, I'd like to think it was the 'decent' part of my personality. Before she left us to go back to Medical, Nikki sat outside with me and stared at me with those lovely, trusting eyes. 'Y'know,' she said softly, 'you're the nicest person I've ever met.'

That stirred my emotions even more and made me tear-up a little, but I quickly explained it away as some grit that had got into my eyes. These women looked to me for strength, calm and a sense of safety. I was a lifeline in the turbulent, crashing waves of their hectic and traumatic lives. I was someone to cling onto for a while; someone who'd be nice to them. I couldn't *cry* for them – not in front of them. If I did it would reinforce a desperate situation, *their* desperate situation. They needed someone to pick them up off the floor, to shelter and tell them – show them – 'It's OK now. You're safe. Nobody is going to hurt you again. I'm here. It all stops now.'

Just 'being there' for them saved lives. Talking them out of suicide; giving them hope. Did it make my sentence worth it? Definitely. Did it change my life for the better? Absolutely. Should I have got a shorter sentence? No. I needed to see this and to be a part of all of it to know who I really was and – given that I'd left my own girls behind – whether I could truly like myself again.

28

AUTHOR, AUTHOR

'I want your visits with my girls supervised from now on!' my ex-husband had snarled into the phone early in the piece.

'They already are,' I snapped back. 'You know those six Corrections Officers who man the Visitor Centre? They aren't cardboard cut-outs.' Honestly, the guy could drive me completely nuts at times.

There were multiple skirmishes like this during which he tried to control what happened to me behind bars by interfering with my access to Shannyn and Sarah. I fought tooth and nail to keep regular contact with them, though I was only allowed a paltry thirty-six hours a year in addition to my two twelve-minute phone calls per week (six minutes per daughter). It seemed incredibly punitive considering I was a non-violent offender.

My ex-husband, I'm sure, saw me as nothing more than a convicted criminal trying to call the shots on parenting from prison. But as far as I was concerned the issue wasn't about a mother's right to see her children – it was about the children's right to see their mother. He didn't seem to understand that.

'Oh yeah, great,' he'd say, 'I'll bring them to see you so they can have barbecues with the murderers and armed robbers.' I do understand that having had no contact with prisons before he had every right to be concerned, but he didn't give allowance to the fact that I naturally would also share that same concern and would never endanger them.

I made a point of never complaining to the officers about him. I didn't need to – they figured him out all by themselves just by watching him. All the women in the unit were like family to me so they knew about my problems with my ex-husband and word got around among the people on their visitor lists, too. He would sit in the Visitor Centre and try to bad-mouth me to the mothers of other inmates. 'Kerry is this' and 'Kerry is that', he'd say. But they knew better.

'Oh well, Kerry just helped my girl get parole,' they'd respond. 'She's getting out next month. Please thank her for us.'

Before too long my ex-husband had created so much unnecessary drama about visitation that Brendan Money decided to step in. Beginning at the next visit, the girls' father was forbidden from entering the Visitor Centre at all. Instead, officers stopped him at the front gate and escorted

Shannyn and Sarah in to see me. This was a huge deal and had never happened before: the moment the officers took possession of the girls, they were legally responsible for them. Every time the girls visited from then on their father had to sit outside in the car park while they spent time alone inside with me.

I was keenly aware that I wasn't the only parent in DPFC who struggled to keep relationships with their children alive, let alone in bloom. A lot of the women faced similar difficulties; an unreasonable and uneducated family member who thought taking children into a prison visitors' centre would expose them to harm. With trained Corrections Officers watching their every move – along with their access-starved mothers – there are few safer places for a child to be. There had to be a way to point this out to thick-headed spouses and ex-partners, so finally I came up with an idea and went straight to Brendan Money.

'There are a lot of people who aren't seeing their kids because it's thought the prison isn't a safe place,' I pointed out.

'Yes, I know,' he said.

'Well, we've got to make them aware somehow, so I'll write a children's book but I need you to pay for it and publish it.'

'Kerry, one day you're going to realise that you don't run this place,' Brendan replied with a smile on his face.

'That's fair enough but in the meantime I need you to support this book.'

He did.

207

With the encouragement of my adorable friend and tutor Carolyn Beasley and the wonderful Michelle Gale from the Parenting Program in the prison, I set about writing a book called *Shannyn and Sarah Visit Mum*. We decided it should be a colouring-in book that not only engaged and educated the children of female inmates, but helped inform their fathers or carers. The idea was that if you were the wife or partner who ended up in prison you would be given the book to sit down and read with your children while they coloured in. The story took them through each step of what to expect during a visit to DPFC: how the officers were friendly and there to help, why Mummy had to dress in a special green zip-up jumpsuit, how the sniffer dogs were very busy hounds who would never hurt a soul. I envisaged pictures of the dog squad coming into the Visitor Centre and the smiling officer talking to the kids: 'This is my work dog so he's not allowed to be touched.' By the time a child started visiting prison they shouldn't be surprised or frightened by anything. It was a friendly book and I loved writing it, but since I was barely capable of drawing stick figures I needed to find an inmate to illustrate it. A woman named Donna Parsons said she was a handy artist.

I didn't know it at the time but Donna was a former professional wrestler from Wales who was known in the ring as 'The Welsh Dragon'. She was serving a twenty-three-year sentence – one of the longest in Victoria at the time – for the murder of her husband. He had been having an affair with a girl called Kerry who had long dark hair – just like little ol' me – so muscle-bound Donna convinced two mentally challenged hit men that her husband was hurting her. One day when Donna was out with the kids, the hit men ambushed him with a crowbar and a knife and he bled to death inside the family home. To set an alibi, Donna – who stood to gain $1 million in life insurance – sent her two young children in first to find Daddy's body. I wasn't Donna's biggest fan from the very beginning, but after she started working on the book we became legendary mortal enemies for the rest of my sentence. Her main problem was that she couldn't bring herself to draw a smile.

'Donna,' I said as she started sketching out pages, 'why do all the mothers and children look grief-stricken?'

'What?' she snapped.

'They all look like they've just been told the world is going to end! This is supposed to be a happy book, with a positive message that makes the kids feel reassured about coming in here,' I pointed out.

'Yeah, I know that.'

'Well, do you think we might be able to turn those frowns upside down?'

She didn't take my constructive criticism very well. Pretty soon it was on.

'Oh, you're going to take over and do everything yourself, are you?' she said, fuming.

'What's with the frowning, desperate-looking people?' I replied. 'It's a fucking kids' book, not the *Australian Police Journal!*'

Donna wasted little time in getting personal. 'I think your kids are better off without you.'

'Well, I think that dog you've drawn looks like a fucking horse!'

That was it: I had criticised Donna's drawings so she downed tools. 'I'm not touching this book,' she said. 'You're a fucking bitch, Tucker.'

Thank Christ! While I wasn't thrilled to have made a bitter rival out of a wrestling champion, I was relieved that she wasn't going to stuff up the book anymore. Little did I know a familiar figure would do his best to ruin the process anyway.

Tania Herman kindly finished the illustrations – complete with grinning mums, kids and officers. Unfortunately, because of her high profile, we couldn't put her name on the cover to credit her with bringing some happiness to the project. But the book did bear my name – my first ever published work – and the title celebrated the sacrifices Shannyn and Sarah had been forced to make because of my mistakes. The prison ordered 10,000 copies, which were to be stocked in prisons, barristers' chambers and legal offices throughout Victoria. Then my ex-husband found out about it and was not prepared to give his permission to have our girls' names used. His purported reasoning? 'People will find out who they are and they could be in danger.'

Seriously.

From where I stood, though, it was purely about ensuring I did every day hard. It was clear I was achieving things within the prison, which meant I quite possibly was going to be a different person when I got out, so he wanted to pull the strings whenever he could. He wanted permission for this and permission for that. I was devastated at the prison – we all were – when Brendan Money said we were going to have to pulp 10,000 books that were meant to do nothing more than make thousands of children's lives easier. I almost wept as he told me the news in his office.

'What a terrible, terrible shame,' I said.

Thankfully Brendan knew how good an idea it was and came to the rescue. 'Just change the names,' he said, 'and we'll print the book again.'

The next time the girls came to visit I held them close and told them what had happened. 'We can't use your names in the book,' I said. 'But you can pick any other name so long as it's not your own.' They conferred for a minute and came up with a solution.

'I'll change my name to Shannyn,' said Sarah.

'And I'll change mine to Sarah,' said Shannyn.

I laughed out loud and hugged them tight. In the end they picked the names of their cousins and then changed them again, and nowadays *Rhiannon and Sasha Visit Mum* is still found in prisons and legal firms in Victoria.

'Mummy, I've missed you so much, when can you come home?' Rhiannon asked.

Mum looked sadly at both of them and said, 'I hope it's very soon too but it won't be before Christmas. It might take the judge a long time to decide when I can come home.' Sasha was more interested in the green

*jumpsuit that Mum was wearing. 'You look like a
Teletubby, Mum,' Sasha laughed.*

*Very soon the visit was over. Mum kissed them
both and said something she used to say to them every
night: 'I'll always love you both more than the stars in
the sky and the fish in the sea.' Rhiannon and Sasha
smiled and knew that Mum was still Mum, and they
would be back to visit again very soon.*

If only that part were true.

After three years behind bars my weekly visits with
Shannyn and Sarah had become monthly, and sometimes
even further apart. Eventually – as their little lives filled up
with friendships, sporting commitments, outings, hobbies,
birthday parties, sleepovers and school – I would be lucky
to see them once every two to three months. There was no
point fighting it, and the daughters I'd once had an almost
physical attachment to became distant facsimiles. They
were my 'prison babies'.

When they did visit it would be for three hours. Sometimes, if they'd been out to a party with their father the
night before, Sarah would just go to sleep in my arms. Quite
a few Sunday afternoons were spent holding them in silence,
which was OK because there wasn't a great deal for us to talk
about. I couldn't say anything about their dad, but to them
he was the centre of their universe and they were forever
bringing him up. They'd talk to me about their friends but
it'd go in one ear and out the other. I didn't know those

mythical kids so I didn't really want to hear about them; to me it was just a wasted conversation. I couldn't gel with the girls' social lives or even their schoolwork. Although prison visits were meant to bring us closer, the reality was they underscored just how far we'd drifted apart.

I would still speak to them on the phone twice a week for six minutes each, but that became weird, too. Strangely it was over the phone that I really noticed them growing up – more so than during personal visits. At first they were tiny, squeaky little mouse voices that sounded frightened to be on the phone to someone in a prison. It made it feel like *they* might be in trouble, and a prisoner was going to tap them on the shoulder. The whole six-minute thing was a nightmare, too. I'd try to coax them into a conversation and at the four-minute mark they'd finally start to loosen up, and I'd have to say, 'Oh, sorry, kids – we're going to have to wrap it up in a minute or so.' They must have felt like I was some oddball psychiatrist: 'Tell me everything. OK, time's up!'

As time wore on they grew into their voices. The squeaky mice had morphed into nine-, ten-, eleven-year-old children. I went from being greeted as 'Mummy!' to 'Yo' and 'Hey' and even 'Wot?' But I could always tell how they were feeling. I had developed a kind of bionic ear that could detect minor variations in the soundwaves they emitted. I could press the phone to my ear in a way that I could almost see them. I always knew when they were trying not to cry, when they were really happy or if they were just having a bit of a nod at my joke. I knew their voices better than anyone in the world. I still do today.

I had to get used to the reality that other women had filled in part of the gap that I had left in their world. I knew when their father's girlfriend had been over because they'd come into the Visitor Centre with bows in their hair and I'll always be thankful to her for that. Other times I'd know that they'd stayed over at his later girlfriend's house after a night out because they'd come in looking like little rag dolls in slept-in clothes. No matter how they presented, though, the painful fact was their lives were moving on without me.

Although the visits were infrequent and the six-minute phone calls could be strained, there was a way that at least I could feel connected to the girls that I had complete control over. Every day I would sit down in my cell and write them a card that contained a new joke. After I burned through all the joke books I could get my hands on, I put word out among the program officers that I needed more. Before I knew it I had a pile of books in my cell. I'd spend all the money I hadn't used for my phone calls on stamps, cards and pens at the canteen.

I sequenced the cards, too. In the very first ones I wrote, 'Today I thought of you 100 times.' The very next day I told them I thought about them 101 times, then 102 times, 103 times ... right up until I was thinking about them more than 1600 times a day.

It wasn't until years later that I found out how much it had meant to them to go to the mailbox every single day and find a card waiting for each of them, and they have kept every last one of them all of these years.

29

SNAKES AND ANZACS

When architects sit down to design a prison they don't stroke their chins and ponder ways to make it a little more comfortable for the inmates, so it's infuriating when you hear people on the outside carry on about how prisons are just like holiday resorts. 'Oh, I tell you,' self-described 'taxpayers' will often say on talkback radio or in the beer gardens of the nation's pubs, 'these bloody crims are living in near luxury with colour TVs, sports equipment and even bloody swimming pools!' Inevitably they'll all draw the same conclusion: 'Some of these so-called prisons are more like five-star hotels!'

It's infantile and it drives me insane.

The truth is the concrete pool at DPFC was built mainly so that in the event the place caught fire the fire fighters had a sporting chance at dousing the flames before a full-blown human catastrophe unfolded. We lived so far out in the backblocks that there was no other decent water supply should a proper fire take hold. The idea that we sat sunbathing around the pool with daiquiri in hand was preposterous.

In summertime the prison was as hot as anywhere else in the state, and then some. Whenever it hit 40 degrees Celsius in the city it was 52 where we were. We had no air conditioning of any description and outside the dry, hard-baked ground was mostly unmolested by trees, so there was virtually no meaningful shade throughout the entire complex. Even in the event a half-hearted breeze managed to start up after dark to take the edge off the overnight swelter, we couldn't leave our doors open to welcome it in. We were locked in our stifling concrete boxes from 7pm during the daylight-savings months. But thank *God* we had that glorified fire hydrant-cum-pool so 300 women could frolic with giant beach balls, have hysterical super-soaker fights, drink cocktails and playfully spring off a pink diving board!

For the record, being in prison is not like being in a five-star resort. It's like being in a prison.

Winters were just as uncomfortable, only in reverse. Prisons aren't insulated any more than they are well ventilated and the besser bricks in the walls might as well have been giant ice-cubes when the mercury plunged. We weren't permitted to have fans or heaters because of the fire risk. Not one of the doors in the prison fitted flush to the ground, nor were they sealed with weather strips, so if it was bitterly cold to begin with, it became near Arctic when wind whistled over the plains of Deer Park, under your cell door, across the lino and straight onto you as you huddled shivering under your blanket dressed in prison tracksuit and dressing gown.

During one such frigid winter, however, we were unexpectedly gifted a reprieve from our state of near-hypothermia. A team of workmen arrived in the prison to carry out an upgrade to the Programs building where we typically had psych appointments, pre-parole appointments, counselling and the like. The appearance of men – civilian men in flannelette shirts wielding tools, shovelling, sawing and hammering away – was an obvious drawcard for the women, and while my interest was also piqued by the blokes, my eye was taken by something even more alluring – a beautiful two metre by one metre mound of sand.

When civilians or contractors enter a prison in any capacity, extremely tight security is put in place. Large cyclone wire fences go up around the worksite so there can be no interaction, and officers are stationed down there to keep a general eye on what's going on. But I'd already fallen deeply in love with the pile of sand and had a plan for our future together all figured out.

While most prisoners might look at sand and yearn for the beach, I took one look at it and longed to be a bit warmer at night. Since a few of the girls were already drawn to the building site to ogle the workmen, we started forming groups of ten to twelve women to mill around near the fence, chat a little and strike up a conversation with the officers.

'OK,' I'd whisper to a couple of the girls, 'you guys go over and have a chat to that officer and don't forget to ask how his little boys are going.' Then I'd get another couple of girls to distract another officer with some interesting inquiry or other, and so on until the cyclone fence wasn't being watched as closely as it might have been. The sand pile sat just on the other side of the fence – close enough for us to reach through and grab big handfuls to shove into the blessedly deep pockets of our tracksuit pants.

We had already organised for some of the inmates who were particularly good at sewing to cut metre-long strips of fabric in a range of garish colours and wait for our gritty, ill-gotten booty to arrive back in the units. Slowly, a range of brightly coloured, sand-filled, hand-sewn door snakes started to appear throughout the otherwise grey prison buildings. This went on for two weeks. We'd wander down to the worksite and start talking to the officers: 'How's your day going, Mr Bruce? How are the kids? Bloody cold, isn't it? B-r-r-r-r! Listen, if I bring you some visitors' lists could you help get them done quickly?'

Meanwhile, behind him, ten girls would reach through the wire fence and pluck fistfuls of sand from the pile before heading back to our snake assembly line. It was the opposite of *The Shawshank Redemption* – we were taking soil back *into* the units. When the pile was all but gone, however, the officers figured out something was up and the questions started. The workmen wanted to know where all their sand had disappeared to and the officers sure as hell did, too.

'OK, what have you done with the sand?' they demanded to know.

'Why are you asking us?' I replied. 'Obviously those workers have used it all on the new Programs building.' But apparently the men hadn't even started mixing concrete yet. 'Well, maybe the wind blew it away then!' I suggested helpfully, palms upturned. 'I don't know. Why are you asking us anyway?' Pretty soon some damning, irrefutable evidence was presented. A lady from the Better Pathways Building Program had periodically been taking progress photographs of the construction and in the background of her pictures a virtual time-lapse history of the great sandy mystery had been unwittingly catalogued. Although none of the shots captured any of us in the act of reaching through the fence or stuffing sand into our trackies, they clearly showed how the pile steadily diminished over a fortnight.

'So, if the workers aren't using it,' the officers wanted to know, 'who is? And why?'

And just like in *The Shawshank Redemption*, the whole prison was put on lock-down as the shit hit the fan. Suddenly it was no joke and the prison administration was determined to get to the bottom of it – pronto. The way they put it, 'If a whole mound of sand can disappear from this prison, then obviously a prisoner can, too.'

'Uh oh!' I thought. 'We've got real issues now.'

But by that stage it was too late. All of the units and every cell had its own door snake. And they weren't shy, timid or camouflaged reptiles either: these things were crafted out of lime green, orange or bright yellow fabric, and adorned with silly, googly stick-on eyes or little moustaches, forked tongues and dopey-looking smiles. People used to get all manner of things sent in for their crafts and hobbies so there was no shortage of things we could use to really pimp up the snakes.

We remained in lock-down for the next two days while every cell and unit was thoroughly searched, and the dog squad was brought through to systematically sniff every millimetre of the prison. Not one of them found a single grain of the missing sand. Yet every time an officer or dog entered a cell or walked through any number of doors in the units, Giuseppe the moustachioed door python or Greg the pale blue 'special needs' snake would be staring up at them through a set of wobbly eyes. We even had snakes dangling off the back of delivery buggies, just hanging out and hiding in plain sight. They became known as 'fuck you snakes'.

After a while the panicked investigations died down but the puzzling case of the disappearing mound was never solved. Years later, I detailed exactly what happened in front of Brendan Money in a way I couldn't have fathomed at the time of the Great Sand Heist. Apart from it being hilarious in hindsight and a nice win against the system, the whole episode resulted in a massive bonus for the inmates by fulfilling its original intention: from that time on we were a lot warmer when the winter winds blew in. The irony is I've been to one or two resorts and five-star hotels in the years since my release and not once have I encountered a door snake. Funny, that.

*

While the manufacture of 'fuck you snakes' had been an illicit industry, there was no shortage of sanctioned, organised enterprises at DPFC to keep the women occupied and 'contributing to society' in some small measure. Nowadays I'm reminded of it every Anzac Day when I pause to remember not only the fallen but also the women who are incarcerated throughout Australia. If you've ever been approached by an RSL member outside a train station or stopped at one of their makeshift tables outside a shopping centre to buy a little plastic pin-on badge for Anzac Day, it's more than likely an inmate had her hands on it long before you did.

Every January, women in the prison would be assigned work sticking Anzac badges onto the little commemorative cards for volunteers to sell to the public. About five months beforehand the girls would get boxes and boxes of these badges and bits of card – hundreds of thousands of the bloody things. It was done inside a shed at the height of summer. If you're looking to place a bet on two women belting into each other, just rock up to that shed after about three hours of work. It was so hot and mundane that someone inevitably snapped. And these women were paid at the lowest rate in the prison of $22 per week. I, by comparison, was one of the lucky ones with the highest pay of $36 per week for my job as peer support worker.

Less fraught but no less challenging was working in the prison 'garden'. I used to wonder why they even bothered since the soil there was as hard as cement. The only place where grass grew – and even then it struggled to survive – was a little patch in the middle of the compound. Yet as an inmate you could attempt to do some 'gardening' if you so wished. When I first arrived in prison, a major furniture manufacturer was using prison labour to have its wooden chairs sanded before they were sent somewhere else to be finished. And I don't mean in a proper workshop with power sanders and ventilation shafts – women were literally rubbing back raw wood by hand with bits of sandpaper. That scheme was shut down after a while because prisoners started getting respiratory illnesses thanks to all the sawdust and flecks of sandpaper they were inhaling every day.

In addition to being skilled at hand-sewing, quite a few of the girls were absolute whizzes with the sewing machines, so there was also quite an industry at DPFC churning out tracksuits for the men's prisons. Then there were the jobs that kept the prison itself ticking over; women worked in the kitchen chopping vegetables, others delivered the food to all the units on the back of a little buggy. There were billets who were the overall keepers of the various units; responsible for the food ordering, for the chemicals to clean the linoleum floors, and so on. Some girls were simply cleaners whose job it was to keep places like the Visitor Centre shipshape.

One of the quintessential prison jobs was working in the laundry. It's also one of the most trusted positions. My friend Sue, who lived with us in C2B, worked in the laundry and through her we usually got the drop on whether a girl was about to re-enter the prison. The laundry was something of a filter and a weigh station in the ebb and flow of human flotsam between us and the outside world. Sue was part of a chain of steps involved in accepting new or returning inmates. Typically when someone leaves police holding cells, for example, the prison knows they'll be arriving and whether their clothing size is small, medium or large. Based on that, Sue would be told to prepare a box containing a pair of socks, a bra and a tracksuit. Laundry workers also usually knew the inmate's name because they are generally processed into prison clothing first before they go off on the other admission steps like psychiatric evaluation and medical assessment. So, with Sue in the laundry, and by parsing other administrative information that would find its way out, she'd come home to our unit and say, 'Guess what? Glenda is on her way back.' Or, 'You won't believe who you'll be seeing later today!'

And first thing every day I would start my job. As a peer support worker my duties were anything but mundane. Sometimes I could find myself emotionally sanding back a chewed-up human being; other days it was like sewing someone's shredded heart back together a little or pulling pins out of her soul. Sometimes it was all I could do to keep from crying.

30

SOFT UNDERBELLY

Brushing up against notoriety is par for the course in prison. Almost everywhere you turn you'll bump into someone who has made headlines for all the wrong reasons. Still, it's strange to think I shared a couple of close links with the late mass murderer and notorious gangland boss Carl Williams. Firstly, Carl and I were both investigated by the ladies and gentlemen from the famed Purana Taskforce. Secondly, we both at one time or another had to put up with Carl's excruciatingly painful ex-wife, Roberta.

When Roberta arrived at Deer Park after being charged with credit-card fraud she had yet to be immortalised on the small screen in *Underbelly*. She was, however, already a household name in Victoria thanks to her maniac ex-husband's penchant for slaughtering people in order to stay atop the state's blood-soaked drug-dealing pile. Melbourne's gangland war was the biggest story in the country and its cast of shady characters was plastered across the pages of *The Age* and the *Herald-Sun* almost daily. Everyone knew who Roberta was. Although she didn't require protection, she was a high enough profile crim that she was kept in the slot until management figured out where best to place her. The first time I met her was on an otherwise quiet Sunday afternoon in the Visitor Centre.

I had fought very long and very hard to have Shannyn and Sarah visit with me alone – completely free from interference from my ex-husband or anyone else. Those precious hours together were almost at the spiritual centre of my life; times when I could just be Mummy and attempt to nourish the strained bond with my girls. The Visitor Centre was a sacred escape hatch.

Then Roberta turned up.

I was sitting outside in the sun with Shannyn and Sarah when Roberta sauntered past with her own daughter in tow. Her gorgeous little girl had her hair in braids and someone mentioned how nice they looked. 'Yeah, fucking oath. It'd wanna look good – that shit cost me $1700,' Roberta bragged in a loud, hacksaw of a voice.

My girls looked at me with a mixture of alarm and confusion but Roberta just continued spouting obscenities like she was on the set of a hip-hop video shoot. 'The fucking dog motherfuckers have got me down in the slot because they're so fucking worried about what might happen if they put me on the compound. Fucking stupid cunts have got no fucking idea . . .'

By now the girls were completely shocked by the angry, fetid invective that poured out of Roberta's mean little sewage pipe of a mouth. So was I. 'Come on, girls, let's go inside for a while,' I said, taking them each by the hand and ushering them into the Visitor Centre building. 'Don't worry about that lady, she's silly. I think she's a little bit angry to be honest and doesn't really understand what she's saying.'

Internally I was fuming but I kept a calm and happy face on for the rest of the girls' visit. An hour or so later Roberta and I were locked in a holding cell together, waiting to be strip-searched and returned to our units. 'You must be Roberta Williams,' I said flatly.

'Yeah, you probably knew that though, eh?' she said, clearly delighted by her C-list status.

'No, I didn't know that,' I said. 'I was just guessing. But since we're acquainted now, let me tell you that after the language you used in front of my little girls, my ex-husband will probably stop visits. He will stop me from seeing my children because they will go back and tell him what you were like with your "fucking cunt" this and your "dog motherfucker" that.'

'I'm . . . I'm fucken Roberta Williams!' was all she could manage in response.

'Well, I'm Kerry Tucker!' I explained.

'So? I was married to Carl Williams!'

'I was married to Colin Tucker!'

'Who the fuck cares?'

'That's my point exactly, sweetheart. Now, if you ever do that again in the Visitor Centre, I'm going to let everyone on the compound know that you have just risked their visits with their children. You will become an endangered species overnight and you will never see the light of day for the entire time you are here. Do you need me to go over that?'

I had a huge heart for the run-of-the-mill, overlooked, traumatised, abused and forgotten drug addicts who no one gave a thought to. The likes of Roberta Williams? I had her in my crosshairs right from the word go. Her notoriety didn't stir any feelings of respect in me. On days like this I would have to remind myself that not too long ago I was just a lonely girl in Robinvale looking forward to basketball practice or forcing myself to read *The Hobbit* – now here I was threatening Roberta Williams with protective custody. My life had certainly seen some twists and turns in recent years.

Eventually Roberta was moved out of Isolation and onto the compound but she was far from the hard-as-nails gangster's moll you'd have expected. When she wasn't curled up in a ball crying, she was whining or demanding extra attention because, y'know, she was Carl Williams' ex-wife. She even had the audacity to beg me for help. 'Kerry, I've got to be transferred to Tarrengower,' she'd sob. 'You've gotta help me. I'm not coping.'

'No, I don't actually,' I was pleased to inform her.

Although I had made a solemn vow to help every woman I could in DPFC, there were some exceptions to the rule and Roberta was at the top of the list at that time. I outright refused to render her any assistance whatsoever – such was the anger I felt at the slightest hint of losing contact with my girls. The 300-odd women in DPFC shared an ironclad understanding about the Visitor Centre. It was hallowed ground where any kind of bad behaviour – swearing or even the slightest negative vibes – was strictly forbidden. It was a refuge where prisoners could concentrate on trying to be Mum for a few precious hours a week. By arrogantly putting that all at risk Roberta had placed herself outside the circle of trust and privilege.

It wasn't that I had a vendetta against her, it's just that her demands for attention paled alongside the genuine needs of other women. I was in Medical one morning to visit with a young girl who'd been raped the night before she was brought into prison, and found Roberta sitting at the front door crying. 'It's harder for me. I'm Carl Williams' wife!' she sobbed.

'Ex-wife, sweetheart,' I reminded her.

Eventually Roberta felt so threatened by her own celebrity she decided to get herself a minder. Amanda was a six foot tall, thin, ageing prostitute from the mean streets of St Kilda. She was known for wearing rollerskates and tiny little shorts as she glided up and down the red-light pavements selling drugs. We called her Deals on Wheels, which she thought was fantastic. Roberta ended up in the same unit as Amanda and one day it appeared they'd become Siamese twins. Roberta refused to go anywhere without her.

'Amanda, what are you doing following *her* around?' I asked one day.

'She needs a shadow, Kerry,' Amanda said matter-of-factly.

'No, she doesn't! No one gives a stuff about her. Tell her to fuck off.'

Then the truth came out. Amanda revealed that Roberta – the influential ex-wife of a multi-millionaire mega-gangster – had promised to buy her a beautiful house the minute she was released, only if she served as Roberta's private bodyguard for the remainder of her sentence. I had never heard such nonsense before. 'Um, Amanda – think about it!' I said. 'She's in here on credit-card fraud.'

'Yeah, so?'

'It's a fair indicator that she doesn't have any money. You're not getting a house.'

Six months later Roberta was released from DPFC and a year or so after that the rest of Australia was spellbound by actress Kat Stewart's portrayal of her in *Underbelly*. If I'd had anything to do with it, Kat would have won the Gold Logie for that performance – she played Roberta to a tee.

There were other inmates I struggled to extend the hand of empathy and kindness to. Some of the women in Protection were the most hated criminals in Australia. Their crimes were considered so deplorable and unforgivable that it was feared 'regular' inmates might kill them on principle the first chance they got. The pariahs in Protection had variously committed acts of cruelty and violence against kids but the deepest loathing was reserved for those who had murdered children. The most notorious among these was Donna Fitchett.

Donna, a nurse from the Melbourne suburb of Balwyn North, had gone through a divorce in 2005. She told her two little boys, aged nine and eleven, that they were going to go on an exciting holiday but needed to drink special medicine so they didn't get 'air-sick' on the plane. After giving them an overdose of a powerful sedative she suffocated them. As a peer educator I was one of only a handful of inmates who had any contact with Donna inside DPFC while she was awaiting trial. The Protection Unit is an impenetrable concrete cage and any time its residents are taken to the Medical Unit, the rest of the prison is locked down. The more I got to know Donna, however, the more I wondered whether people needed to be protected from her.

Donna was an extremely cunning woman who filled her lonely days by playing legal and procedural games with the prison authorities. She had an area all to herself but one day she decided she wasn't going to remove her rubbish anymore. The officers refused to remove it too so at the height of this stand-off I was summoned to Protection to sit down with Donna and try to find a solution.

'This is going to get you nowhere,' I told her, gesturing at the filth that was piling up around her. But she just fixed me with her dark eyes and smirked, like I had no idea what she was up to. Donna was a master of vexatious litigation and a keen student of Corrections' own operations manual.

She would launch legal proceedings the moment anyone strayed from the black-letter interpretation of prison procedure. She once sued Corrections over an unauthorised urine sample – not because she was taking drugs, but because they had apparently collected the sample incorrectly. She took the matter all the way to court and won! That pissed off the officers even more. I tried to talk to her about the wisdom of it all: 'Donna, you're in a concrete cell and you only see two people each day – the officers – and they hate you. You're only making it worse for yourself.'

But Donna was playing at a longer-form game. She was trying to get the courts to rule that she was insane so she'd get to serve her time in a mental facility that was a lot cushier than the Protection Unit at DPFC. In my mind I thought her mental state was cut and dried. 'If you can do that to your own children,' I thought, 'then you have to be insane.'

'I really shouldn't be treated this way,' Donna complained during one of my visits.

'Donna, what you have to realise is I'm not judging, but in the officers' minds you outright killed your sons.' As soon as those words left my mouth I wished I could suck them straight back in. It's a hell of a thing to talk to a woman about the defenceless children she has killed. But thankfully Donna remained composed. 'What you're doing,' I continued, 'is making yourself look very sane because no one else has sued Corrections and gotten away with it the way you have. You're looking very clever, and very calculating I might add.'

Perhaps it was because I was straight with her or maybe it was due to the fact no one else would even talk to her, but Donna started requesting my presence whenever she was at loggerheads with management, during any appearances in Governor's Court and after every time she attempted suicide. Not that she was fooling me. Donna had been a nurse so she knew a thing or two about emergency medical care. Whenever she'd have a go at 'suicide' she'd carefully nick a vein and press the buzzer, or she'd do it five minutes before muster. In any case she was always saved by officers long before she was at risk of bleeding out. If she'd been serious about meeting her maker, she'd have cut herself properly at 1am and just lain down to die.

The last time I saw Donna Fitchett she appeared to be in a wistful, reflective frame of mind. She was talking about the breakdown of her marriage. I was sort of listening and sort of not, but before I knew what was happening she was describing things I just did not want to hear about.

'NO!' I snapped and walked straight out of her cell. When the officers approached me in the hallway I was doubled over with my hands on my knees and hyper-ventilating. 'Are you OK, Kerry?' one asked. 'What on earth has happened?'

'No, no. Nothing. I'm OK, but I'm telling you now I can't do this anymore. I will not go back in there with that woman. It's over.'

I'll never know if Donna knew what effect that little conversation would have on me, but it was so shocking it almost took my breath away. I kept picturing my girls' faces.

'NO!'

I didn't want my loving thoughts of Shannyn and Sarah floating around in this poisonous atmosphere. I didn't want Donna to see their faces in my mind. I felt that if she looked deep enough into my eyes, she'd see them because I could. I kept blinking the girls away, further and further until their images were pressed up against the back wall of my skull where I stored all the boxes. Safe from Donna and everyone else.

Eventually a jury found that Donna was indeed criminally insane and she was sentenced to twenty-seven years in Thomas Embling Hospital (a high-security forensic mental health hospital), where apparently it was quite pleasant by comparison to DPFC. She appealed that sentence, however, and was sent back to serve it in maximum security in Protection at Dame Phyllis. Had she stayed at Thomas Embling she would have been able to walk the grounds and have visitors any time she liked. Not that I think anyone would have come.

31

TIME

There's a reason they call it serving time. After you've been stripped of everything else, time is all that society can take off you as punishment. When you keep handing your time over day after day and year after year, however, it creates a black hole into which other things disappear: your relationships, your dreams, the person you once were. And when every day is a replica of the last – the same walls, same people, same clothes, same routine – the passage of time becomes harder to measure. That's until the calendar throws up cruel reminders that make you sit and contemplate the time you have lost. You'd think Christmas Day would be the worst. It's not.

Christmas was all about getting in touch with children and family. Since the thirty-odd women in the C Units all wanted to use the phone at once on Christmas Day

I started a ballot system where the officers would draw our names out of a hat. It was always rigged in my favour but no one seemed to mind. I'd have six minutes on the phone with each of my girls to find out what Santa had brought them and what they were doing for the day. 'I-love-you-Merry-Christmas-darlings-and-Mummy-will-speak-to-you-soon-bye!' And then Christmas parenting was over for another year. When everyone's phone calls were done with, we were locked in while the skeleton staff of officers had their own lunch.

We'd sit around in the cottage and have our 'family' lunch. We were given Christmas ham and Sue would have ordered a chicken to cook. Later, when the officers had finished lunch, the girls from other units would come and visit and sometimes exchange gifts from the canteen. Tania even fashioned a Santa outfit one year. Each passing Christmas got a little easier. The first one I was distraught and would have done anything to stop thinking too much about what was happening on the outside: excited children burrowing under the plastic tree at dawn, the squeals of delight as presents tumbled from coloured paper, the bustle of getting ready for Christmas lunch, the drunken afternoon rituals of dancing, napping or fighting, and the tears of children who, when the excitement had dimmed, realised how much they missed their mum. After a while, though, it just became another day to get through.

Boxing Day could be a bit of a drag and New Year's Eve wasn't too bad because at least the women could watch the fireworks on TV, not that I ever did – I made a promise to myself that I'd only let myself enjoy spectacles like that when I was welcome to do so live. Then New Year's Day would lumber in like an elephant and crush you up against your cell wall. To most people 1 January is a time of new beginnings, new goals, fresh challenges and the end of bad habits. Even to some inmates it spells the beginning of the end of their sentence. But to the long-termers it was just the start of another gruelling year in the black hole. It is the worst day ever.

I'd walk out of my cell on New Year's Day and picture a giant ladder suspended in the air with 365 rungs that reached up through the clouds. I couldn't even see where it ended, but I knew I had to fight, struggle, claw and squirm to pull myself up every single rung one at a time. At the end of the year, if I made it to the top, I'd get to slam my flag into the summit on 31 December like a solo mountain-eer and say, 'I fucking survived!' The next day I'd have to squeeze past the elephant to get out of my cell where a new ladder would be waiting for me. I'd hate to think what it was like for some of the *really* long-termers.

Women who were serving heavy sentences – ten years or more – were afforded a special kind of respect from the other inmates. It wasn't 'respect' for their crimes (which were often heinous), nor was it because they were seen as hard-arses or women to be feared – it was simply an acknowledgement of the enormous price they were paying. Three thousand, six hundred and fifty rungs. Seven thousand, three hundred rungs. Ten thousand, nine hundred and fifty rungs. Mary was one such woman with a long climb ahead of her.

An Egyptian woman, Mary had been forced into an arranged marriage and had two young children at the time she started having an affair with her husband's brother. When her husband was found burned to death in his car in St Albans, a suburb north-west of Melbourne, police thought it was suspicious that he was still wearing his seatbelt. That and the fact toxicology showed he'd also been drugged. They quickly had Mary and her lover in their sights.

Another breakthrough came when Mary took herself to the Western Suburbs Hospital to have an abortion. The police quickly got a warrant to take a DNA sample from the aborted foetus, which conclusively proved the victim's brother was the father. This provided prosecutors with a motive. A jury found them both guilty of murder and they were each sentenced to twenty-one years. It was the lead item on the 6pm news so everyone in the prison knew of Mary's fate. It was about 8pm when she was brought into A5.

Normally, at that time of night, A5 was a noisy and rowdy place with women yelling abuse and threats at each other from their cells, demanding cigarettes or just being stupid. But when Mary came in, the place was deathly silent. You could have heard a pin drop. My cell gave me a window seat to the mournful procession. No one said a word – not the officers, not the inmates. All we could hear were footsteps as Mary was marched to a cell and the door was closed behind her. Then for the next three or four hours the only sound we heard was Mary sobbing to herself at the very bottom of seven thousand, six hundred and sixty-five rungs.

Like the rest of us, though, the people left behind in Mary's life were also sentenced to suffer. I took time to get to know her and discovered her children – a boy and a girl – were about the same ages as Shannyn and Sarah. They had essentially been orphaned by Mary's murderous acts, given that their dad was dead and their mum would be in prison into their adult years. They wound up in the care of their paternal grandparents who asked the courts to prevent Mary from seeing the children at all. They also planned on taking her kids to Egypt, where they wanted to have them included in an old-world ritual that Mary objected to.

'What can I do for you, Mary?' I asked as she sobbed in her cell one day. 'You're going to be here for twenty-one years and I need to be able to help you adjust to that.'

'Can you just enable me to see my kids for a little bit longer?' she pleaded. 'That's all I ask.'

Putting my experience in the Family Court into practice, I got the officers to download an ex-parte agreement that we were able to file and stop the grandparents taking the children out of Australia. I got to know Mary's side of the story. She had undergone that same ritual herself when she was eight years old and was forced to marry someone she didn't love. Don't get me wrong, murder is murder and it is wicked and evil, but when you live in a place where every second person is a murderer you don't differentiate between who is a good murderer and who is a bad murderer. As a peer support worker it was important to see the woman and not the crime.

On 1 January 2007, I walked out of my cell and looked up at the ladder in front of me. It was different: a bit shorter and it didn't disappear into the clouds. I realised it was the last New Year's Day I would spend inside DPFC. I pulled myself onto the bottom rung and started climbing.

32

DAY RELEASE

In the final few months of their sentences, DPFC inmates are normally sent to Tarrengower, where specially designed work-release programs with an array of local businesses help prepare women for reintegration into society. Even though my security rating had been dropped to the lowest 'C' shortly after my sentencing, I decided to remain in maximum-security for the entirety of my sentence regardless. I wasn't going to a prison farm – or any farm for that matter. Besides, who was going to represent the DPFC women and write their letters if I was living among chickens and cows and working at some health retreat way up near Bendigo?

Over the years a firm called Wyndham Legal Service at Werribee had heard dribs and drabs about an inmate at Dame Phyllis Frost Centre who was doing paralegal work and advocating for prisoners' rights. My latest efforts in trying to get domestic violence programs into the prison had also made some waves, and when one of the women from DPFC Education approached Wyndham Legal Service to see if they'd be happy to take me on as a day-release placement they said, 'Yes, absolutely.' The problem was protocol: I was still a maximum-security prisoner so I technically didn't qualify for that kind of leave. The conundrum was put to Brendan Money and the governors to consider. 'It's never been done before, Kerry,' Brendan told me, 'but leave it with me and I'll see what we can do.'

A delegation from the prison drove down to the law firm's offices and gave them a detailed briefing on what I could do, what I couldn't do and how transgressing from the carefully planned day-release framework would likely see their premises surrounded by two dozen police and Corrections Officers. The governors paced it out and decided that on top of working inside the Wyndham Legal Service offices I would be able to walk to a nearby cafe and back. After about three months wading through red tape I was all set to go for work release two days a week. Each morning before being driven down to Werribee by one of the officers I was strip-searched and handed my civvies: a skirt, a blouse and my heels. Oh God, I was so glad to be back in my heels.

As much as I enjoyed going out and working I felt like a total fraud. I wasn't the wonderful, vivacious person who the people at the corner cafe thought was the new lawyer at the legal firm. I was a maximum-security prison inmate who was pretending not to be, and the deception by omission made me uncomfortable. While it had been designed mostly to punish me, prison had in fact improved me as a person. I was imbued with a steel-reinforced sense of right and wrong, of personal dignity, self-identity and the value of being honest and forthright in every aspect of life. I very much wanted to tell the lovely baristas that I was no barrister but, ironically (and understandably), Corrections regulations prevented me from telling the truth. The people at the law firm knew, of course, and they were lovely to me.

I manned the phones, helped manage the office calendar and welcomed the clients – many of whom were just like the people I'd lived with for the previous four years: the marginalised, the downtrodden and the addicted. Sometimes we'd get chatting. 'Well, you just wouldn't have any idea of what I'm going through,' they'd say.

'Yeah,' I'd respond, 'I sorta do.'

While work release was designed to help prepare me to re-enter society, I found it confusing. In prison the lines are black and white but beyond the razor wire it was a blur of colour. The more I spent my days playing paralegal with a nice bunch of professionals, the weirder it felt making the transition back to my friends, the murderers. I'd return to the prison each afternoon to good-natured remarks from the officers: 'Where are you going to start your own law firm, Kerry? In here or out there?' Back in the cottage the girls would have cooked dinner and I'd sit down and tell them all about my day.

I found I was taking a bit of the law firm back to prison and a bit of prison out to the law firm. The biggest change was that by working outside the prison between 9am and 4.30pm two to three days a week, I was no longer able to fully perform my peer support role. Suddenly I wasn't quite such a crucial cog in the prison machine and I was by no means a bona fide person in the community either. I had entered a never-never land. One day I almost slipped between these two worlds and could have disappeared forever.

A condition of my day release was that I had to be back at DPFC by 5pm each day. An officer would collect me from Werribee at 4.30pm as regular as clockwork. One day, however, 4.40pm came and went. Then 4.45pm, 4.50pm . . . 4.55pm. 'Oh my God, where are they? I'm going to be in serious trouble!' As 5.15pm came and went, it became clear they'd forgotten me. I imagine there are any number of maximum-security inmates who might have seized the opportunity to escape, to head for the hills and never come back (or at least until they were captured, as escapees always are). But not this little black duck – I was desperate to get home before 7pm muster. Sue was cooking her world-famous curried chicken. I picked up the phone and called the prison.

'Good afternoon, the Dame Phyllis Frost Centre.'

'Hello, it's Kerry Tucker here.'

Silence.

'Hello.'

'Yes, hello, did you say Kerry Tucker?'

'Yes, I did.'

'*Our* Kerry Tucker?'

'Yes, one and the same. I'm on work release in Werribee and it appears someone has forgotten me. Is Mr Wood there?'

'No, Mr Wood isn't here, can someone else help you?'

'Well, anyone who has an interest in bringing me back to prison would do.'

There was a pause. 'Oh yes, certainly. Oh dear, stay right there on the line, OK?'

'No worries. Remember, it's me ringing you, so obviously I'm not going anywhere, OK?'

'Yes, of course, Kerry. I'll find Governor Blyth. One moment.'

'Thanks.'

Click. Music.

Click. 'Wayne Blyth.'

'Forget something?' I asked.

Chuckle, chuckle (from both of us).

'No. Not really. They're on their way,' he said, before adding, 'Stuck in traffic.'

'Yeah, of course they are.'

'They won't be long, Are you OK there?' he asked.

'Yep. If I'm not here when they arrive, I'll be enjoying happy hour at the pub around the corner,' I quipped.

'Just go easy on the table-top dancing will you?'

'I'll wait here then.'

'They won't be long, OK?'

'No worries, I'll see you soon and damn lucky for you that I will.'

'You reckon? Seeya.'

'Bye.'

I could hear the troops rallying in the background before I'd hung up. It was 5.40pm by the time they arrived, and I finally made it back to the prison around 6pm. My permit had expired an hour and a half earlier. Technically I had become an escapee at 4.31pm. When I returned, the officers in the Medical Unit were all leaning up against the front desk with wide smiles on their faces.

'Geez,' I sighed loudly as I walked past them, 'do I have to run this place from the outside as well?'

The next morning I passed Governor Blyth on the compound.

'Fine time for you to be getting home last night, young lady,' he said with a cheeky grin.

'Shoe sale at Myer. You're lucky I came home at all.'

The truth was I had been terrified and was desperate to get back.

But when I returned, despite being surrounded by women I knew and even loved, I felt very lonely. With no one else to turn to I sat at my computer and poured my heart out:

So, I've sort of gone from the mover and shaker – the head or representative of the unit – to a woman with no voice. This just happened to occur on a day when out on day leave, the staff wanted me to go to the local restaurant with them for the farewell lunch for the principal solicitor who is leaving. Of course, I couldn't be included in this either so I had to sit out the back of

the law centre while the front door was locked
and read magazines, waiting for them to return.
This was just how it had to be done so I would comply
with my permit. However, it was a day where I had
lost my voice and position in my unit . . . I had to be
excluded also from being included in a grown-up
situation with people in the outside world. I literally
didn't know where I belonged, if anywhere at all.
I was in a complete state of suspension, waiting to be
received from my old world to my new world. Not yet
there. I really felt for a moment that I belonged in no
world . . .

The people around me also have their own anxieties
about my release. People take me aside to ask me,
'What will you do when you leave?' I can't answer
that question. I've always solved that for them. I've
always been able to answer their questions or resolve
their issues. I'm not used to not having a solution for
them. They ask and I don't know the answer. It's like
I'm abandoning them, leaving them behind. It's a
difficult situation . . .

Some women in here have actually shed a tear at
the thought of my departure. This changes me, moves
me . . . Officers are even stopping me, asking me what
the prison will do when I leave. What the women
will do. It's an amazing thing. I didn't think I'd made
such a difference because it required no effort from
me. I just did it. Like it was made for me. Prison and
the women fitted me like a glove, as if this place was

tailor made for me. Different officers know exactly how many days I have left. I didn't until the other day, when they told me.

And it had scared me to death.

A few days later I phoned the girls. Sarah was great but Shannyn was in tears. She had something to tell me.

'Promise you won't get angry, Mummy,' she sobbed.

'I promise, darling.'

'Well, I'm worried about telling you . . . I, I don't know but I'm worried about you coming home!'

'Oh, Shannyn, that's OK, sweetheart . . .'

'What I mean is that I don't want to live with you when you get out. I want to stay with Dad.'

(Oh. Ouch!)

'I don't want you to be angry at me,' the poor girl cried into the receiver.

I did everything I could in six minutes to reassure her that she had nothing to worry about, that I would never take her away from her father and that nothing could make me stop loving her more than the stars in the sky and the fish in the sea. 'Shannyn, it's going to be fine, sweetheart. And I'm not angry with you. I understand.'

When I hung up I felt like I had been winded. I was slipping out of the picture even before I'd got the chance to be part of it again. The more I thought about it, however, the more I realised I didn't need to just say that I understood,

I needed to *really* understand how Shannyn felt. There was no point blaming anyone or being resentful – I simply needed to accept that this was my little girl and she was scared about staying even one night away from her dad. That's how much the sentence had actually disconnected me from her.

A few weeks later Shannyn and Sarah came to see me in the Visitor Centre – for the very last time. Sarah was ten and Shannyn was twelve. The tear-streaked little girls I'd crushed to my chest in that very room for the first time nearly five years earlier were long gone. They had been replaced by a pair of tweenagers who had endured half a lifetime with their mother behind bars. The visit didn't seem such a big deal – until they left. When the door closed behind them I felt as if an umbilical cord had been severed and for the first time I had to resist the very real urge to run after them and get them back.

I had developed a life with Shannyn and Sarah that had taken place exclusively behind the razor wire. They had become, in the most real sense, my prison babies, and even though I would soon be going home, I felt as if I had lost them forever. It was as though they had died, and I mourned their deaths into the lonely hours of the night.

33

FREEDOM

In prison, women can become twice the person they are. Literally. All of a sudden they get off the drugs and become addicted to soft drink and confectionary instead. Junk food is consumed by the bucket load in DPFC, where the dietary staples are potato chips, chocolate bars, Coke and Red Skins. It was nothing to see girls pack on forty to fifty kilos in a year or two, and some women literally doubled in size. Although I, too, put on weight I was fortunate that I spent my days on my feet scurrying from one unit to the next so I didn't swell up as much as others did. Besides, the girls in my unit ate quite healthily thanks to Sue's amazing ability as a cook. Generally speaking, though, DPFC was a fat farm.

When women started to shrink again it was a clear sign they were about to be released. You'd be in prison with them for years and for the last month and a half they'd disappear into the gym every day to whittle away the Deer Park kilos. 'Yep,' I'd think, making a mental note, 'she's getting out soon.' Inmates also had to complete a number of programs and jump through some administrative hoops in order to qualify for parole – Drug & Alcohol Support, Housing, Parole and the like. As a result little clues to their imminent release would be broadcast over the prison PA. 'Smith to Programs' and 'Smith to Reception. Smith to this, that and the other.' I'd turn to my friends and say, 'Jenny Smith is getting out.' Now the PA was squawking my name.

The situation in my unit was like an open wound. I'd be sitting and laughing with the girls after dinner when suddenly it would fall silent because everyone was aware I was leaving in a few weeks and nobody really knew what to say. Far from anyone being happy about my impending freedom there was a sense of sadness and dread because we knew the familiarity and comfort we shared was about to be shattered. The next morning the bloody PA would start up: 'Tucker to Programs.'

As the final days of my sentence ticked by I felt as though I was see-through. I struggled to be heard, like a song on the radio that was fading out. Soon enough a new tune would be playing and I wouldn't be around to hear it. The girls in the unit started discussing who was going to fill my bed when I was gone. 'I know of a girl who has come into A5,' I offered. 'She's going to be here for a while and is nice enough. Maybe you should think about getting her in.' But my once powerful voice had become a distant echo of itself. After all, I wasn't going to have to live with the newbie. I had quickly gone from being someone who felt as if she practically ran the prison to being voiceless, and it came as a massive shock. It's not that the girls were being cold or nasty, I just wasn't relevant to life anymore. My song had fallen silent. That's when I started to realise I didn't want to leave prison. Not ever.

It's customary for long-termers to be given a farewell party on their final day. We chose a barbecue. For my last hurrah I stipulated that it would only go ahead if the prison officers were invited too. That raised a few eyebrows as it had never happened before, but I said it was either that or nothing. For years I had refused to abide by the old-school code of 'us and them' so there was no way I was going to start now. It was my final, parting gesture to acknowledge that the officers had been part of my prison journey, too, and many of them had been supportive and helpful – particularly in regards to my daughters. We ended up having a wonderful barbecue and, one by one during the afternoon, about twenty officers dropped by to spend time with me and wish me well. Towards the end Miss Johnson – the Scottish woman who had been the first real officer I encountered back in 2003 – asked if she could speak to me privately in my cell.

'You sure can,' I said with a smile.

As we stood face to face, Miss Johnson cleared her throat and pulled eight paperclips out of her pocket. 'I can't give you a gift or do anything special, so these paperclips are all

I can offer you,' she said in her lilting Scottish accent, and started clipping them together one by one. 'The first five are for every year you impacted by being in here [clip]. And this one is for Shannyn [clip], this one is for Sarah [clip] and the last one is for you when you get out tomorrow, Kerry [clip].'

I was so touched I wanted to give her a big hug but that was against prison rules so I just gave her a tear-stained smile instead. I still have the paperclips.

Later on Brendan Money called me to an office in the new Programs building. 'Kerry,' he began as he stood up, 'I just want you to know . . .'

They were the only words he managed to get out before I burst into tears. 'I don't want to leave!' I cried. 'Please! I don't want to leave here. Let me stay. I can stay here and everything will be OK. Take it off my parole . . .'

Brendan Money had been the first male since my father who had invested anything in me unconditionally. He was patient, he listened to me – even when I was frustrated and at my worst – and he went out of his way to place immense trust in me. He was a towering figure of goodness and decency in my life and I never wanted to let him down. Bizarrely, by leaving prison, I thought I was somehow betraying him and everything he had done for me.

'Kerry, you're leaving. Tomorrow!' he said, trying to sound excited for me.

'I don't want to go!' I said in between sobs.

'You've got to go home. We have to let you out.'

'I don't have a home. This is my home.'

Brendan Money sighed as I tried to pull myself together. 'We've never had a prisoner like you before, Kerry,' he said quietly. 'In a way we'd love to keep you but you have paid your debt. You have served long years in this place and helped thousands of women in the process. I want to say thank you for everything you have done. I will always remember your time here as the Kerry Tucker era. But now you get to leave and make a good life for yourself and your girls. They need you, Kerry.' I couldn't speak through my tears so we left it at that. But I refused to say goodbye to him.

The following morning, on 9 November 2007, I was walked to the gate by a group of women including Renate and her little boy, who was now a spirited and hilarious four-year-old. 'Where's Aunty Kerry going?' he asked with all the innocence of a child whose entire world was a maximum-security prison. Even sadder was the fact I didn't really have an answer for him. 'Where *am* I going?' I wondered. For 1645 days I had thought of Shannyn and Sarah as little pots of gold who'd be waiting for me at the end of my sentence. But there I was, somewhere over the rainbow, and they were nowhere to be seen.

Their father had thought it might be too much for the girls to deal with a reunion seconds after I walked out of the prison gate, so he decided I could take time to get together with them properly – and on my own – in a day or two. After a tearful farewell at the gate my sister Cheryl, family friends Joylene and Sharon and other family members collected me and I was driven away from Deer Park for the last time. It felt as if I was in a dream.

An hour or so later we arrived in Docklands on the edge of the Melbourne CBD for lunch in a waterfront restaurant. Members of my family were there, food and wine was ordered, photos were taken and people fussed over me. I had never felt so weird in my life.

Cheryl had booked us into a plush, expensive apartment in Docklands, and Joylene and Sharon had gone to the trouble of buying me my favourite Oscar de la Renta perfume and a beautiful white dressing gown to wrap myself in. It was a lovely gesture that was meant to make me feel extra safe and comfy but I just felt like a freak instead. I dearly missed my prison clothes. Soon I picked up on the fact that my family were talking about people I didn't even know. A lot had changed in the years I was away. For one thing Mum had died, but there were also five babies born who I had never met. Cousins and nieces had married people I didn't know. I realised I was the stranger in my family.

As the sun arced towards the west I started to grow very anxious. At 3pm I looked at my watch and got a massive jolt. 'Shit!' I said. 'I'm going to miss muster!' From that moment all I could think about was what the girls in the unit would be up to. What were they cooking for dinner and what was the newbie like? I was dying to sit down in the cottage and tell them about the dressing gown and the apartment and all the freaky new relatives who might as well have been extras in a movie. I felt trapped between my longing for my prison family – women I knew warts and all – and this strange new crowd who I didn't really know from a bar of soap. I was thankful for the wine, however, otherwise I don't think I'd have ever got to sleep. I sort of missed my cell.

The next day Cheryl – the most generous person I know – offered me the use of a chauffeur-driven car to go see Shannyn and Sarah. I met them at the gates of Swinburne University in Lilydale where Carolyn worked. It was neutral turf and my ex-husband drove us all to Chirnside Park Shopping Centre, reminding me that, 'You've got two hours', a little as if I was still under guard and wearing my prison blues. The girls and I piled out of the car and once alone, we just stood and cuddled. The air seemed fresher but after five long years, it was awkward. They were thrilled to see me but realised it was only for a couple of hours. There were no tears of joy, just a warm feeling of having them in my arms.

We made a bee line for the shopping centre – ground zero for re-entry into lost motherhood. And then it started. 'Mum!'

And it didn't stop. 'Mu-*uum*!'

'Mummy-yee!'

'Maaa-aaa-aarm!'

'Mummmargghhhh!'

'M-U-U-U-U-M-M-M!'

If the little buggers weren't badgering me every five seconds they were fighting with each other. Fighting! They played up and squealed and complained in the middle of the shopping centre so the whole world could see what a crap mother I was. I could not believe how lost I felt. I could easily manage the affairs of 300 criminals but out here I had no moves. 'Oh, Jesus Christ! What am I supposed to do with these little people?' I wondered. 'Fuck! They're annoying the shit out of me.' Fortunately I knew better than to go with my gut instinct, which was to tell them both to shut the hell up or else they might wind up in the slot. Instead I figured if I could get food into their mouths they'd at least quieten down temporarily. Five minutes later we were hunkered down over McDonald's in the Chirnside food court.

As the girls silently munched on their Happy Meals I could finally take a moment to just look at them and absorb what was happening. 'I am with my girls,' I thought with a mixture of wonder, pride and sheer terror. 'We are free in the world together. My God, they're beautiful. I love them so much.'

Just as I was feeling something approaching calm a woman appeared at our table from out of nowhere. 'Hi Sarah! Hi Shannyn! How are you going?' she almost sang as if she was Mary Poppins herself. The girls mumbled a greeting through their McNuggets. Apparently the woman was a friend of their father's. Then, as suddenly as she'd appeared, Poppins turned on her heel to leave – without once saying a word to me or even letting her eyes stray in my direction. But she knew very well who I was. She made it two steps away before I was on my feet and in her face. 'If you want to talk to my children in front of me you will introduce yourself because I am their mother, whether you like it or not. Understand?' Poppins looked like a deer in the headlights as I pulled my best pencil lips and prison glare.

Golly gosh, this whole 'fitting back into society' business was *hard*!

About ten minutes later the girls and I were browsing in the aisles at Big W. 'I really like that top,' Shannyn said as she ogled a T-shirt that had sparkles sewn into it. Naturally, I wanted to please her – I'd have bought her a pony and carriage if they'd had any in stock. The next thing I knew we were lined up at the check-out with a clutch of clothes for the girls with money that had been deposited into my account by Cheryl. When we were second in line I noticed the EFTPOS machines were now different from how they'd been when I was sent to prison. I just knew I'd get to the check-out and appear a complete idiot. So, as the lady in front of me was paying her bill, I peered over her shoulder to see if I could work out what to do.

'Excuse me!' the woman said sharply as she spun around to face me. 'Are you trying to get my credit-card details?'

'What . . . the . . . n-no! I was just . . . just – *No!*' I stammered as I shook my head. Day two. Out with the girls for the first time, and the police were going to come and take me back to prison by 5pm. 'Look, I've just never used one of these machines before and I was trying to see how it was done,' I explained. 'Honestly. See – I've got my own card!' I waved it and gave her a big smile. I may have figured out how to work the EFTPOS machine, but I still came out looking like a complete idiot in the process. Later in the afternoon as I sat and watched the girls on some play equipment I overheard snippets of the conversation going on around me among the other parents:

'What about if we do it next Saturday?'

'Why don't we get everyone around next week for a barbecue?'

'Can you bring the lawnmower around? I desperately need to cut the grass.'

'You know what Bill's like!'

'Yeah, well, why don't we meet at five o'clock at that little bar in Burnside?'

I sat there and marvelled. 'Jesus! All these people have got a life.' I was sitting among them but I might as well have been from another galaxy. I didn't have a lawnmower. I didn't have a house. I didn't have a barbecue that people could come around for. I didn't know that little bar in Burnside and I had no idea what Bill was like. I didn't have any friends – not out here anyway. My girls were still fighting and complaining, which was pissing me off, and it was almost time for muster.

34

DAY THREE

It had taken just two harrowing hours to realise the girls were completely settled with their father, whereas I was about as stable as the *Fairstar* in a cyclone. I had to get my act together. First I needed a place to live, which was easier said than done. When an inmate leaves prison you are required to provide Corrections with the address of where you will be living. My house in Healesville had been confiscated and sold off long ago so I simply didn't have a home to go to. Nothing. Fortunately the Prison Housing Service was there to help – they directed me to a putrid little one-bedroom unit on the ground floor of an apartment block that was swarming with addicts and dangerous ex-criminals.

When I arrived at the address in Ascot Vale I was dismayed not only to discover it was a 'prison release block' but that I was the only female tenant. The rest were men who had just been let out of Barwon Prison – home to people like Carl Williams. The fear that gripped me as I walked up the path only intensified when I pulled the flimsy apartment door closed behind me. The place was a dive. It was old, it stank and it was 'furnished' with dilapidated items you'd find on the footpath during a council rubbish collection. There was no TV, the kitchen tap didn't work, the pongy mattress was covered in stains and – worst of all – the lock on the door was about as secure as a plastic latch on a child's jewellery box.

I didn't sleep a wink that night thanks to my neighbours knocking on the door and the window. They weren't hoping to borrow a cup of sugar, though – they wanted to know if I needed to score, whether I had any money or if I could help them get drugs. I missed the C Unit like a baby bird who'd fallen out of its nest. In prison I had been 100 per cent safe from every threat in the world and I had slept like a log almost every night for the past four-and-a-half years. I couldn't believe the Prison Housing Service would turn me out with nowhere to go and then put me in a dangerous and stinky cesspit crawling with desperate men. As soon as the sun came up I phoned my lovely friend Carolyn and organised to meet her at Swinburne University.

'Oh my goodness! How are you feeling, Kerry?' she asked as a taxi dropped me at the main gate of Swinburne's Lilydale campus. I must have looked totally wrung-out and dishevelled. 'I'm feeling much better now,'

I said, 'because I know I'm never, ever going back to that shithole of a unit. They can put me in prison again first.'

Carolyn had arranged for me to move into the university's student accommodation. This not only provided me with an escape from *Casa del Crim* in Ascot Vale, it put me close to where Shannyn and Sarah attended school in Lilydale. The accommodation itself was lovely – a bright and tidy one-bedroom unit with a comfy bed – but the best feature was the security swipe card, which no one could get into the building without – the next best thing to being locked up. The campus itself was spread across carpets of lush green grass and it even had its own lake. I was in the best of both worlds; I felt secure in my little 'cell' plus I had a sliding door that opened onto a step where I could sit and watch ducks paddle across the water.

Without Carolyn's help, and of course Cheryl's, I would have struggled to find my feet in society. She had lobbied hard to secure a job for me at Swinburne University three days a week, and the cost of the accommodation was deducted from my salary. I had also accepted a receptionist's job at my old day-release placement at the law firm in Werribee where I would be working on the other two days. My first role at Swinburne was administration in the writing department where I'd done my Master of Arts. With the degree under my belt I was also invited to do a PhD in writing. I was extremely grateful but I quickly realised I was also the university's golden girl and something of a research project to the professors. They had never had a PhD student who had come to them from inside a maximum-security prison before, so my job and study there had a feeling of *quid pro quo* about it.

I'd spent enough time in prison to know that day three of an inmate's freedom is the hardest. Carolyn seemed to twig to this, too. At the end of my third day she turned up at my room with a bottle of Fifth Leg sauvignon-blanc as she'd promised she'd do years earlier in prison. As we sat together on my little step and looked out towards the lake, I began to debrief with her: my family had all returned to Mildura (at least the ones I actually recognised); I'd had a nightmarish afternoon with Shannyn and Sarah, and realised I'd had better understanding and control over them while I was in prison; I'd had a run-in with a snooty woman I didn't even know, and I'd narrowly escaped from the scary slums of Ascot Vale without being robbed or worse.

'Do you know what, Carolyn?' I said as we watched a pair of ducks glide over the lake's glassy skin, 'if you weren't here I would call my dealer.'

'Kerry! You don't even take drugs!' she said with a snort. 'What *are* you talking about?'

It was a good question and it made me realise how ingrained in the DPFC drug culture I had become, and how I fundamentally understood what the women meant when they said day three is too hard. At that moment I felt the word 'institutionalised' was probably a good fit for me. 'I miss prison, Carolyn,' I said. 'I guess what I'm saying is if I had a dealer I would definitely have called them by now. I totally get what the girls mean when they say that. All this other stuff: life? It's just so fucking hard.'

One of the pre-release programs I completed in prison was run by a group called the Self Help Addiction Resource Centre, or SHARC. Of course, I wasn't addicted to anything – not if you don't count my addiction to prison itself – but I really liked their concept. The SHARC program was concerned with re-establishing relationships ahead of a prisoner's release. It made me think about my relationships in more detail and how some of the structures in prison made it impossible to have real relationships until I had actually been released. Now that I was out I was finding out just what a big deal this particular aspect of 'freedom' could be. So, I was surprised when, just eleven days after I was released, SHARC invited me to give a speech at a workshop being held in an old church in St Kilda.

A lot of the people in the audience were struggling with depression, addictions, mental illness or all three. But knowing I was a clean-skin, the SHARC people asked me instead to talk about how prison can have a positive impact on a person. That was easy, because I truly believed it could, providing women were properly supported inside. I had seen it happen to others and I was living proof of the edict myself. I stood at the front of the old church and talked about resilience, the strength of the human will and the value of never giving up on yourself or others. I spoke about the programs that are available in prisons to help people deal with their problems and improve themselves. I told stories, cracked some jokes and gave examples of what life in prison could be like and how you could always find positives in every situation. I was told afterwards that it was a great talk.

That was pretty much the first such speech I had ever given. I had learned that the fear of public speaking is so common it has its own word: glossophobia. In the years ahead I was to discover I was the opposite of a glosso-phobe. I love public speaking and it is one of the few things I know I am really good at. I'm in my comfort zone behind a microphone and in front of a group. I can read an audience and know when to shift gears to keep their attention, or, if they're confronted by the subject matter, when to tell a joke or make an aside to release the tension. I didn't know it then but the SHARC talk was the first of hundreds of public appearances that would eventually lead to an audience with the Governor-General. If only it was so easy talking to my own daughters.

It quickly became obvious that years in prison had largely dismantled our relationship. All those long after-noons in the Visitor Centre, all the cards I sent them, all the phone calls I made . . . none of it could alter the fact I had left them. Now that I was finally 'back', the reality of the damage that had been done hit home hard. I felt more like a step-mother to the girls than anything else. Or an aunt – Aunty Mum. I could be wooden, unsure and stand-offish with them. I didn't know their friends, I had never been to netball practice – in fact, I hadn't seen them outside of prison walls since they were little girls. None of this was their fault; they were innocent victims of my terrible behaviour and the tragedy was they continued to be – for a very long time.

It took a full five years for us to rebuild our relationship. It wasn't the same as before, and we had to put ourselves back together using emotions and character traits that had been buckled and bent by the experience. I had spent my entire sentence trying to prove that I wasn't going to harm them, break their trust or disappear again inside a green jumpsuit in a prison Visitor Centre. I never counted on feeling like I would get out and sometimes decline to see them in favour of a night on the town.

Another relationship that had been intrinsically altered by prison was the one between me and men. Where I'd once tended to be subservient to men, I emerged from prison as a single-minded, almost ruthless piece of work. I wasn't exactly a man-eater, but I would date guys and as soon as I was bored or had something better to do, I'd drop them like a hot potato. Sometimes men would ring or send me an SMS the next day. I'd write back with all the charm of a robot: 'What are you texting me for?'

'Oh, I just really like you.'

'So?'

That attitude had been cast in the emotional furnace of prison. Make no mistake, women who are locked up for years *will* have lascivious thoughts about some of the male officers, but you dare not say it or show it – not unless you want to risk getting killed on the compound. In a women's prison, lustful thoughts must be locked up between an inmate's ears. You clamp down on your sexual impulses – hard. Suppress, suppress, suppress. By the time you get out, all of that pressure crushing down has forged your sexuality into a blunt but effective tool. You are so used to stomping on the feelings that might have given you butter-flies in your previous life, caused you to blush or made you want to give yourself to someone completely. What's left is animal instinct – a wanton, self-serving sexuality. Well, that's how it was for me anyway.

Not that I didn't have a good time with some guys. There were a few I got close to. There was one man I had a bit of a thing with for a while. He was a senior figure at one of the banks and we'd seen each other a few times. We met up after work quite late one night and ended up back at his place, a lovely apartment in St Kilda. About midnight we were standing on the balcony having a glass of wine. 'Hey, did you know that's a corner where ladies of the night hang out?' I asked my date, and pointed to a stretch of the footpath across the road that glowed in a puddle of street light. Before he could answer, a slender figure stepped out of the shadows and leaned into the window of a car that had just glided up like a scene from *Pretty Woman*. I did a double take.

'Rachel?' I called out, causing the figure to look up at the balcony.

'Kerry? Is that you?' a voice replied.

'Heeeyyy, Rachel! You're out? Great to see you,' I said and gave her a thumbs up.

By now Rachel had moved her potential customer on with a firm but dismissive wave of her hand, like a cop directing traffic. 'Come down here!' she squealed. 'Bess is around here somewhere and Jude's just up the road. They'd love to see you.'

I had to turn her down. After all, I already had a date, who was now shaking his head in amused disbelief. Up until then he'd only known me as Kerry the fiery brunette who worked at the uni. 'Come inside and sit down,' I said to him. 'Perhaps I should tell you a little bit about myself.'

He sent me a text message a couple of days later: 'Hey, I really like you!'

I never got back to him.

35

REVLON AND RAZOR WIRE

During my prison years I wrote between 3000 and 4000 parole letters for my fellow inmates, plus thousands of other pieces of correspondence and appeals. On top of that I religiously sat at my computer and bashed out more than 560,000 words in my personal diary and painstakingly kept prison journals. Add that to my Master of Arts in Writing and I generated millions of words inside DPFC, representing many tens of millions of keystrokes.

Four years later I found myself a PhD candidate at Swinburne University of Technology and I had to find a way to turn my journals into a doctorate: a new 'significant original contribution to knowledge'. Obviously my area of expertise was prison and the women inside it, so I felt well placed to take an in-depth psychological look at human behaviour, at community and at women. The question was how to put that original knowledge across in a compelling and engaging way. I couldn't rightly submit half a million unvarnished words straight from the hard drive and expect people to read it, let alone draw nuanced conclusions from my base material.

I had been going from strength to strength as a public speaker at that time. I didn't have a business card or a website, let alone an agent, but through word of mouth I kept getting invitations to speak on issues related to the prison system, public welfare, addiction and rehabilitation. My PhD supervisor at Swinburne, Chris Sinclair, had been to a few of these sessions and one day she came up with a brilliant idea. 'Why don't we make it into a play? Some kind of performance?' she asked. 'That way we can really bring the story off the page and breathe life into it.' I adored Chris, still do, and was happy to do whatever she suggested. The PhD then took on the form of Artefact and Exegesis. The performance would be the Artefact.

'Well, if it's anything like public speaking then I'm all for it,' I enthused and thought to myself, 'This is going to be shit easy.'

It wasn't at all like public speaking and it was anything but shit easy. I decided to call my one-woman play *Revlon and Razor Wire* – a fifty-minute performance featuring twelve important and instructive tales from my time in prison. I explored themes through vignettes that told stories about my incarceration, my sentencing, strip-searches, muster and the harrowing tales of the women I was locked away with, like Janice the Down's syndrome inmate and some of the tragic girls who had died. There were lighter moments, too, like the story of the 'fuck you snakes'. And the play traced my journey from motherhood to maximum security and the girls' metamorphosis from my daughters into prison babies.

The process of preparing to perform the play was incredibly hard. Aside from the writing, script editing, stage direction and props, there was the small matter of the lack of a lectern. While I was somewhat cocky when it came to public speaking, I soon discovered I was indeed a glossophobe when it came to being onstage as a 'performer'. Without a podium to stand behind I might as well have been as naked as during my first strip-search. It took six months of rehearsal to be able to stand still and deliver my lines without veering off to the right or left if there was a chair or a prop onstage that I thought I could put between me and the audience. Meanwhile, *Revlon and Razor Wire* became a big production very quickly.

Before I knew it we had moved from the intimate High School Theatre at Boronia to the famed La Mama Comedy Courthouse Theatre in Carlton, where things really stepped up in terms of production, music, staging and lighting. It was a much more intimate room, too. Overwhelmed by the closeness of the audience I asked that the two front rows of seating be removed to put more distance between me and the audience. I had gone from a super-confident, entertaining, in-control person behind the speaker's lectern to a nervous wreck on the open stage. But I wouldn't trade the experience for anything. One night

I looked out to see Brendan Money was sitting front and centre in the crowd. He laughed extra hard during the story of the Great Sand Heist. Afterwards he came to see me.

'It was fantastic, Kerry,' he said. 'But for some reason I was expecting to laugh a lot more. You're such a funny person.'

'I didn't want to come across like I loved the place too much!' I shot back with a grin.

'Fair point,' he said, 'but we certainly had our moments, didn't we?'

Revlon and Razor Wire wasn't the only time my journals came in handy. In 2011 I was contacted by a TV producer named Lara Radulovich who was in the process of remaking the series *Prisoner*, which would eventually screen on Foxtel. I had never been a fan of the original show but I was certainly familiar with its cult status in Australia. Lara and the series writer Peter McTighe invited me to be a consultant on the remake that was to be called *Wentworth*. They asked me to contribute ideas to the plots and characters, but they also relied on my advice for authenticity. They'd write scripts and send me episodes so I could go through and scrawl notes correcting the writing for lingo and believability. 'This woman wouldn't have said that. That exchange could never happen. This woman wouldn't have acted like that, otherwise she would have gone to Protection. No one talks to an officer like that . . .' and so on. It was a lot of work.

Huge amounts of the show were based on my journals. Bea Smith, the main character, was built around my story, but she was written as a woman who killed to avenge the death of a daughter. The other girls in my unit could tune in and see versions of themselves portrayed by actresses, too.

Watching the show made me miss the women inside even more. Renate Mokbel was the only ex-prisoner I kept in contact with socially, although my best mate Carolyn Beasley was another lasting and constant friendship I made inside prison. Because I was released ahead of Renate I started visiting her terminally ill mum, and she and I became close. On some nights Renate's little boy would stay with his grandma so I would go over there with buckets of his favourite KFC to give him a little bit of continuity from his environment at DPFC. I know Renate would have done the same thing for me had the roles been reversed. Thankfully Renate was back in the community to bury her beloved mother, a day we again spent together mourning lost family. To this day, we both adore each other's children and our prison family bonds will last a lifetime.

Had you told me while I was in prison that I'd one day move back in with my ex-husband I would have – quite honestly – bet my life against it. But desperate times called for desperate measures. In the first few years after I was released my housing situation was very unstable to say the least. At one point – after moving out of Swinburne's temporary student accommodation – I found myself homeless. My ex-husband got wind of this and kindly offered me a place to stay with him and the girls. 'Not like a relationship or anything,' he said.

'You've got that right,' I assured him.

So there I was, suddenly back in a home setting with Shannyn and Sarah for the first time in six years. I spent a lot of time with them and even felt a bit more like a mum. Over a month they started to trust in me again and realised I wasn't going to be hauled back off to prison. Then their father started complaining about what time I got home and how I wasn't grateful, and I was out of there by that afternoon. I didn't realise it then but this crushed the girls. After all they had gone through, it had been hard for them to finally open up their little hearts and invite me in to make myself at home. Then I tipped over the furniture and ran out the door again. To this day, however, I remain extremely grateful for my ex-husband's gesture at the time. It took some guts in front of his new judgemental friends.

The distance that prison creates between people who love each other is just immense. I hate to admit it but there were times when I deliberately avoided the girls. There were also times when I didn't have enough money to be able to do things with them. It made me feel less of a mother than ever. It was easier for me to go out with Carolyn and friends from Swinburne all night instead and let them buy me drinks, switch off and not worry about being a mother. The next morning I would be riddled with guilt and would try to phone them. Sometimes I was able to make it up to them, but not always, and I'd feel as far away from them as ever.

The girls never lived exclusively with me. Their 'home' was always with their dad and although I had ceased being a green jumpsuit–wearing criminal to Shannyn and Sarah, I was definitely more of a side figure than their mother during those years. I slowly worked on rebuilding my emotional life to the point I could offer some kind of stability to them.

While that disconnect started to heal over time, I realised some things that had been broken in DPFC were actually beyond repair and best left as they were: in pieces, never to be the same again. A great example of this is Christmas. Both of the girls are ultra-Christmassy; Sarah even wears a shirt with little Santas on it. She is a full-on Christmas elf, they both are, which I absolutely adore. I don't see them on Christmas Eve or Christmas morning and they always have lunch with their dad – a time-honoured tradition. Interfering with that is the last thing I'd want to do. I don't put up decorations or go overboard with presents and fuss, but I love the fact the girls come over on Christmas night. We have a special dinner and they stay over so we can hang out on Boxing Day. The unspoken message is: 'OK, I'll be a little bit Christmassy with you for one night because that's what you want, but then it's back to normal tomorrow.' The fact is, prison changes you and you never change back.

Unlike just about every other ex-inmate, I was extremely fortunate to fall into a new career in academia. Even though I've worked hard in every role I've held it has never been lost on me that some of the women who waved me goodbye at DPFC would have resumed a life of misery or died after they got out.

At Swinburne University I ascended to the role of lecturer in Media Studies before becoming a receptionist and Freemantle Fellow at the University of Melbourne's Ormond College. I adored the community there. Then, in 2017, I interviewed for the role of Academic Administrator at a college in the Melbourne CBD. Although I felt I'd done quite well during the interview, it must be said nobody asked me questions like, 'Have you ever been convicted of a serious offence?' or, 'Have you spent time in a maximum-security prison lately?' I was quite conflicted because I felt they had the right to know my criminal background but, at the same time, I really needed the job so I wasn't going to shake hands with the dean and the board, sit down and say, 'Hi, everyone, my name is Kerry Tucker and I was sentenced to seven years' prison for fraud.' I decided I would let them get to know me first and then gently bring it up.

That turned out to be easier said than done when I got the job. I was itching to confess but it never seemed to be the right time to tell my co-workers that I used to hang out with the likes of Tania Herman and Donna Fitchett. How to raise the subject? Finally, after a few weeks of indecision, I could stand it no more and one Friday I made myself the promise that I would tell the dean on Monday when I went to work. I'd have the weekend to practise what I'd say.

Before I could learn a word of my lines, though, I was invited out for Friday-night drinks with a few of my new colleagues, and they blurted out that they knew about my time as a guest of Her Majesty. One of the staffers had Googled me apparently.

I was horrified. Would this mean I'd be fired? What did they think of me now? Before any thoughts could spin wildly out of control, they gave me a hug and reassured me that they didn't care. I was so moved I could have cried.

But I still hadn't told the dean, so I spent an anxious weekend worrying about how he'd react. My job was on the line. I barely slept that Sunday night as thoughts about what he might say crashed about in my head. On the Monday morning I knocked gently on his door and asked if I could speak to him. I explained about my past and said that I'd been hoping to settle into the role before letting people know that I was an ex-prisoner.

'Kerry,' he said, 'we all know and no one cares. You were hired on your merit as the best person for the job and that hasn't changed. We think you're amazing.'

'You don't know me,' I replied, grateful he simply accepted me for who I was.

'Well, I look forward to getting to. And if anyone has an issue with you, come to me and I'll sort it out.'

'No, no. That's OK,' I said. 'I really appreciate it but that's not how it works. I can look after myself. I will never cause you any grief but I will deal with people on my own terms.'

Mostly that entailed me taking the piss out of myself. If there was a farewell or someone had a baby and a hat needed to be passed around for the gift, I'd make a crack: 'It's probably best that it's not me!' It was important to try to make people feel at ease. After all, I did go to prison, I did commit fraud and people have a right to feel however they do about that. If people didn't like me for what I'd done in the past, then that was OK. I got it. But I was confident that once they got to know me they'd eventually realise I was no Medusa.

The way I saw it I had paid for my crime and I had proven myself over and over again. I pleaded guilty, didn't appeal my sentence, didn't ask for Legal Aid or community funds for my defence, remained in maximum security all the way without asking for any breaks, reductions or preferential treatment. I earned my degree the same way an outside student would, with high distinctions and a HECS debt to pay off – and managed to do so without the internet. I also worked hard to forge a career and happened to be fun to work with. So, if people still had a problem, I could rest assured it was theirs and not mine.

The notoriety that I could have lived without at work gave me the platform I valued when it came to advocating for women's rights and improvements to the judicial and penal systems. I've spoken at more than 500 community events and worked hard to give women in prison a voice in the community. Women in prison are far and away the most marginalised group of women in Australia and I was only too happy to stand up and speak on their behalf. I know how the prison system works, how the courts work, how the criminal world works and I know how these different threads come together to form a web in which women can easily become entangled. Whenever I speak, whether it's a debate on TV, a talk in front of 200 people or an interview with 100,000 listening on radio, the first thread I pull is making the point that no prison sentence should ever be trivialised. The loss of freedom is huge and it's important to acknowledge that first. Once that's out of the way we can get down to the nitty gritty.

My work as an advocate has given me some incredible opportunities. I have been invited to address the Melbourne City Council with the Lord Mayor, attended a private function at Victoria's Government House with Alex Chernov, the then Governor of Victoria, I have gone to VACRO (Victorian Association for the Care and Resettlement of Offenders) functions alongside the wonderful Justice David Harper, and been asked to be an ambassador for the fabulous community service Wear for Success. I have even volunteered in the courts. A few years ago I was invited to address the State Conference of the Court Network, a voluntary group that provides support for people interacting with the judicial system. The audience included the network's patron and the then Governor-General of Australia Quentin Bryce. I had the pleasure of meeting her afterwards and she asked me what the most pressing concerns were for women in prison in Australia. I told her it was the people who had no business being imprisoned in the first place – people like Janice.

My overarching belief, however, is that prisons do work. Yes, they can work a whole lot better, but I have seen prison save lives. And one life saved is enough. There are many more women who would have been dead if it wasn't for the Corrections system. For the most part, it's not the prisons that break people – it's what happens to them in society. And while I paid a dear price in prison myself, it made me who I am today. And I like that person.

36

MY INSPIRATION

Strolling through the Melbourne CBD one lunchtime a few years ago I found myself in the courts precinct. A surge of powerful emotions flooded back as I realised I was walking over the top of the underground chambers and corridors where I'd spent so much time as an outcast. I paused and stood still on the footpath as fast-moving eddies of office workers swirled past me. Few, if any, of them would have known about the lives that were falling apart beneath their feet right at that very moment. They probably wouldn't have batted an eyelid if a strange-looking, windowless cattle truck powered out of a basement car park in front of them.

I listened to the click of women's high heels on the concrete around me and suddenly remembered the lady in the stylish tan-coloured skirt and the black stilettos

I had spied from a cell so many years earlier. I scoured the nearby footpaths until I finally found the little sub-street-level window near the County Court on William Street. Now I was the carefree woman in heels but was anyone locked up down there? I moved closer and tried to peer in but the midday sun made it impossible to see into the gloom. I was about to call out when I realised I had nothing to say; no assurances, no advice and no comfort to give. If some poor woman was locked away down there maybe she wanted to be left alone. I turned around and resumed my life of liberty.

It's been ten years since I left prison – long enough to know that prison will never leave me. I used to dream about DPFC a lot during my early years of freedom but not so much these days. Sometimes, though, I will still wake up and, for a split second, wonder if I'm back in my cell – and it's not an overly unpleasant feeling. For whatever reason, I thrived in prison, I never felt unsafe there and I was treated well. If I'm honest I'm not so confident about the real world – after all, this is where the crimes are committed, not where they're paid for. I have moved house no fewer than twenty-one times since I was released in 2007 – once every six months on average – which tells me I'm still looking for a place to fit in. But I know this much: wherever I lay my head I want to feel like I am locked in and guarded, if not by another person then by state-of-the-art security. Preferably both.

My current abode is on the top floor of a building right in the heart of the city, where I'm sealed off from the chaos and dangers of the streets below and the miserable place beneath the pavement. There's a twenty-four-hour security reception desk downstairs so there's no way anybody is getting in. You might think surviving prison would make a girl cavalier about life on the outside, but for me the opposite is true. I spent years locked up with women who told me in detail the lengths they would go to in order to feed a heroin habit. As much as I wanted to help them while we were in prison, I'm not so eager to help bankroll the process through having my home burgled and my meagre possessions stolen. I know single-storey houses are the most vulnerable because thieves can go straight through a window, but up at the top of the skyline I'm pretty safe. If ever I hear a noise at night it doesn't worry me. Nowadays I sleep almost as well as I did in prison. I love the fact that both my girls have their own cars and come to Mamma's whenever they like. It was a big moment when, ten years after my release, I eventually gave them their own keys to my place. I finally felt like a real mother again.

I continue to hold my prison years close to my heart and with a great deal of warmth. It's a time of my life that I can't lie about, even if I wanted to, and I refuse to say the platitudes people seem to want to hear from ex-prisoners. Apart from the time spent away from Shannyn and Sarah, I enjoyed it. A lot of the time I even loved it, and part of me will always miss it. Go figure. As a punishment did it work? Hell yes – I was deprived of the most powerful bonds a woman can have – for the best part of five years. But beyond that, my sentence was also the making of me as a person – a better person, I believe, whose own awakening had a positive impact on thousands of women who came through the Dame Phyllis Frost Centre. I was never trying to be a Wonder Woman or set myself up as some sort of Mother Teresa because I am most definitely neither. But the fact remains that prison had a powerfully transformative effect on me – like a lightbulb being switched on for the first time. The glow just happened to spill into the darker corners of some other women's lives as well as my own.

The whole time I realised there was something bigger than me at play, and that was my girls. They went through so much when I was away: teasing, ridicule, name calling, loneliness, plus the embarrassment, frustration and anger that comes with having your mother locked up in prison when you need her most. But they always defended me in the playground, at the park and even against grown women in their own town. So much got swallowed up in the vacuum that formed between us: their first netball game, their first bra, their first period and all the Christmases and birthdays and milestones and relationships. All gone forever. In a way it would have been easier on them if I had died because at least I'd be gone and they could move on. But there I was, always lurking just beyond the western horizon at Deer Park and conspicuous by my absence. I figured the only way they could come back from all of that was if I returned to them much bigger and much better than my sentence was. I believed I could do that and I now feel that in some ways I did.

As well as advocating for the disadvantaged and women in the criminal justice system I have noticed that the desperate and the needy are more visible to me since my time in DPFC. The tragedy of that is I now realise that they are everywhere, and probably always have been. The Taras, the Sharis and the Debbies are on every second street corner. I was standing at a bus stop after work recently when a woman approached and asked if I had any money. I had watched her work her way along the line of people at the bus stop only to be turned down by every single person. Then she was standing face to face with me.

'Have you got any spare change?' she asked. I could tell she wasn't stoned or drunk but she was, most definitely, homeless.

'Oh, sweetie, just let me have a look,' I said and dived into my handbag. I managed to scrounge together the five or six dollars I had jangling around in the bag my girls had given me for Mother's Day, and gave it to her. 'Here you go. Unfortunately it's all I've got but it's yours.'

She looked at me with astonishment and said, 'Wow, you're the nicest person ever.' It broke my heart and reminded me of poor little Nikki with the butchered arms. If that was her response to a stranger handing over a few dollars in change then it spoke volumes for the type of treatment she was used to. I'm willing to bet she was sexually abused as a child. People like to say we live in the Lucky Country, but, the way I see it now, the real luck is what life you get born into.

*

Halfway through 2017 I was asked to give a speech and serve as Master of Ceremonies for Melbourne Inspiration Day – an event where people share and celebrate personal stories about resilience, redemption and, well, inspiration! Because my dear friends from La Spaghettata in Carlton were sponsoring the day, I was thrilled to accept. Shannyn had prior commitments but Sarah said she'd come and see me speak at the conference in Doncaster, so I booked two seats in the front row for her and her thoroughly adorable boyfriend, Tom. I was onstage for three-and-a-half hours as host and occasionally I looked down at the front row and noticed the two seats I'd set aside remained empty. 'Oh well,' I figured, 'Sarah hasn't been able to make it after all.'

Later on it was my turn to speak. 'Sometimes inspiration has to come from something bigger than you,' I began. Since Sarah wasn't in the audience I decided to really open up about what she and her sister meant to me. I abandoned my notes and ad-libbed. 'The biggest thing in my life, what inspires me more than anything else in this world, are my two girls,' I told the room. 'With dignity, grace and strength they went through what no children should – having their mother removed. And it was *my* fault. When I was sent to prison they were ridiculed, they were abandoned, they were embarrassed and they were hurt. But through an innate, dignified resilience they stood tall and waited for me to come back to them. They inspired me every day, right from the very first hour. I will never forget watching them leave the prison Visitor Centre for the first time, flanked by two large uniformed officers and crying out for their mother. I said to them then, "I will make you proud of me one day." They *inspired* me to make that vow and to do everything I could to keep it.'

I paused for a moment and that's when I heard a little sob coming from the back of the room. I'd know that sound anywhere. It was Sarah.

'Have you been here the whole time, sweetheart?' I asked her when she came to the stage to see me at the intermission.

'Yep, we came in just as they were closing the doors,' Sarah replied. 'We didn't realise you'd got us front-row seats so we sat at the back.'

Afterwards there was a question-and-answer session and when that wrapped up I addressed the room again. 'As you know I have two inspirations. Well, one of them happens to be here right now. Would you all please give it up for Sarah, my youngest.'

I asked Sarah to stand up as loud applause filled the auditorium.

'Do you know what, Mum?' she said later when the crowd had thinned and we stepped together into the evening air. 'We really are proud of you.'

Since leaving prison I've been asked many times to give talks about my experiences and what life is like for incarcerated women. But there's more to the story than that; there's the life you have to face when you get out. It's not easy – a lot of things can go wrong, even when you have a job, family and friends. For example, since walking out of

DPFC I've had to contend with chicken pox, pneumonia, and I was bitten on the arse by a redback spider, which required emergency surgery. I've been betrayed, deserted, homeless, financially vulnerable and lonely, and while I've tried to maintain contact with some of my friends from prison it hasn't been easy – many inmates become different people once they leave prison and a lot of them die.

But then again, I've started a new career, thanks to getting my Masters in prison, and have made new friend-ships. I've earned my PhD, I've got to see my odyssey played out on *Australian Story* and I've had lunch with the Governor-General of Australia. Most important of all, though, I have watched Shannyn and Sarah grow into the most beautiful young women. My prison babies may be gone but these amazing creatures will always be my little girls who I love more than the stars in the sky and the fish in the sea.

ACKNOWLEDGEMENTS

Thank you Shannyn and Sarah – for waiting for me, for loving me, for being my daughters. If I had to choose between loving you and breathing – I'd use my last breath to tell you I love you.

Carolyn Beasley – to me you're a beautiful mirror and a lovely shadow; a mirror never lies and a shadow never leaves. Because of you I laugh a little harder, cry a little less and smile a whole lot more. My saviour.

My sister Cheryl – the epitome of compassion, kindness, humility, gentleness, loyalty and patience. I aspire to be like you every day. For never walking away; my saviour also. My mother's protector.

My sister Lynette for being at the end of the phone always. Loyal, kind, funny. For telling me you were proud of me.

ACKNOWLEDGEMENTS

My niece Rachael, for writing to me every single month without fail and feeding me love from the outside.

Joylene and Sharon for supporting me throughout those years and more importantly for being there always for Cheryl. Thank you.

The brilliant Craig Henderson. 'To Paul from Annie.' Thank you for your good nature, sense of humour and hours and hours of calls. You respected my life and nurtured my story. Your intrinsic understanding of another soul is reflected in your beautiful words. I am truly blessed and humbled to know you.

Swinburne University for the opportunities extended: Professor Kay Lipson for paving the way, Professor J. Arnold, Dr K. Vigo and Dr Dominique Hecq for getting me there.

The wonderfully brilliant Dr Chris Sinclair – my friend, my mentor. Thank you for *Revlon and Razor Wire* and for being someone who filled my life with laughter and warmth.

Brendan Money, Paul Galbally, Philip Dunn QC and Dr Paul Brown – I defer to Gandhi: 'Man becomes great exactly in the degree in which he works for the welfare of his fellow men.' You are all great men.

Thank you, Sally, for always sprinkling fairy dust over my girls' hair whenever they visited.

The Women of C2B – Andrea M, Sue F, Wendy S, Jo S, Renate and son – my prison family. Many happy and hilarious times. Sometimes memories sneak out of my eyes and roll down my cheeks.

The women of my time: Caroline, Tania, Emma, Shantele, Shari, Robyn, Lyn (Tiny), Lisa, Angela, Mary, Marty, Kezza,

Jacqui, Sue L, Marie, Denise, Tracey R and so many more to fit here – it was a pleasure.

Prisoners Past – to ensure they are remembered, they are written into these pages so the life of the dead is placed in the memory of the living.

The governors and officers of the Dame Phyllis Frost Centre – Governor Tracy Jones, Governor Wayne Blyth, Officer Steve Kelleher, Officer Gail Johnson, Officer Blackburn, Officer McKenzie, Officer Kump, Officer Bennett, Kathy Katzourakis, Programs Officer Michelle Gale, Salvation Army Chaplain Jenny Hayes, Catholic Church Sister Mary – I thank you for being a big part of my journey through the system.

Penguin Random House – to Sophie Ambrose in Sydney for being one of the nicest people I've had the pleasure to deal with, a funny, warm and caring soul. Consummate professional. To Lou Ryan for always ensuring I felt like an old friend in the Melbourne Penguin family – and for her smile. Jessica Malpass for ensuring her belief through promotion of *The Prisoner* was as infectious as her personality and commitment.

In memory of Michael Maynes. On that last day I had you, my life changed forever. The reality is I will grieve forever. I may not get over the loss of you, but I will learn to live with it. I will heal and rebuild myself around the loss of you. I may or may not be whole again, but I'll never be the same again. Nor should I be the same . . . and nor should I want to be.